KNOWLEDGE AND
THE STATE OF NATURE

Knowledge and the State of Nature

An Essay in Conceptual Synthesis

EDWARD CRAIG

CLARENDON PRESS · OXFORD

1990

Oxford University Press, Walton Street, Oxford OX2 6DP
Oxford New York Toronto
Delhi Bombay Calcutta Madras Karachi
Petaling Jaya Singapore Hong Kong Tokyo
Nairobi Dar es Salaam Cape Town
Melbourne Auckland
and associated companies in
Berlin Ibadan

Oxford is a trade mark of Oxford University Press

Published in the United States
by Oxford University Press, New York

British Library Cataloguing in Publication Data
Craig, Edward 1942–
Knowledge and the state of nature : an essay in conceptual synthesis
1. Epistemology
I. Title
121
ISBN 0–19–824243–3

Library of Congress Cataloging in Publication Data
Craig, Edward.
Knowledge and the state of nature : an essay in conceptual synthesis / Edward Craig.
Includes bibliographical references.
1. Knowledge, Theory of.   2. Languages—Philosophy.   I. Title.
BD161.C67 1990   121—dc20   90-34414
ISBN 0–19–824243–3

Typeset by BP Integraphics

Printed in Great Britain by
Biddles Ltd,
Guildford & King's Lynn

TP

for
H

ACKNOWLEDGEMENTS

I am grateful to many students, colleagues, and friends from various universities in Britain and Germany for their interest in and comments on earlier versions of parts of this monograph. My principal debts can be gathered from the text itself. A number of people have given me the benefit of their native-speaker's expertise over the linguistic data that I refer to in Sections XVI and XVII. Their generous help is much appreciated.

Particular thanks are due to the Leverhulme Trust for enabling me to devote a large part of the year 1986–7 to this project. How much longer it would have taken to reach the present state without such assistance, or whether it would ever have been reached at all, I can only guess.

Finally, my thanks to the editor of the *Proceedings of the Aristotelian Society* for permission to re-use material which appeared in Vol. LXXXVII.

Churchill College, Cambridge   E.J.C.

CONTENTS

I

The standard approach to questions about the concept of knowledge has for some time consisted in attempts to analyse the everyday meaning of the word 'know' and its cognates. Such attempts have usually taken the form of a search for necessary and sufficient conditions which, when measured against our reactions to examples both real and imaginary, match our intuitive ascriptions and withholdings of the title of knowledge. We are to provide, if you like, an explicit intension to fit the intuitive extension.

One might wonder whether, if the idea is to analyse the concept of knowledge, this can really be the right programme. As well as intuitions about the extension of the concept, we seem also to have certain intuitions about its intension, that is to say intuitions about why certain cases do, and others do not, qualify as knowledge. Thus we may feel about a certain example, both that the subject does not have knowledge, and that he does not have it because the truth of his belief is accidental (for instance). The sceptic notoriously tries to show that the two do not mesh: our intuitions about the intension, the conditions of application of the concept, in fact determine a much smaller extension than that which our directly extensional intuitions mark out. If he is wrong, the point needs arguing; if he is right, the question arises: to which set of intuitions should we give priority in order to arrive at the analysis of the 'everyday' concept? Either way, a good deal of work in epistemology and the theory of meaning (which in the light of history one can hardly expect to be uncontroversial) must be done or assumed just to reach the stage of saying that there is such a thing as the everyday concept of knowledge at all, let alone settle any question as to how one should proceed to analyse it. So if the standard approach runs into difficulties—and the work of the last twenty-five years makes it apparent that it does—it is surely worthwhile to try to think of another.

And there is another problem, though in this case it may be less a flaw in the approach itself than a defect in the attitude commonly taken towards it. Let us suppose, however optimistically, that the problem of the analysis of the everyday meaning of 'know' had both been shown to exist and subsequently solved, so that agreed necessary and sufficient conditions for the ascription of knowledge were now on the table. That would be a considerable technical achievement, and no doubt a long round of hearty applause would be in order, but I hope that philosophers would not regard it as a terminus, as many writers make one feel they would. I should like it to be seen as a prolegomenon to a further inquiry: why has a concept demarcated by those conditions enjoyed such widespread use? There seems to be no known language in which sentences using 'know' do not find a comfortable and colloquial equivalent. The implication is that it answers to some very general needs of human life and thought, and it would surely be interesting to know which and how. And the threat, of which some writers have seemed largely unaware, is that the more complex the analyses proferred in response to the flood of ingenious counterexamples (and some are very complex indeed), the harder that question will be to answer.

These two thoughts, that it will do no harm to have an alternative angle on the concept of knowledge that does not start from its supposed extension, and that its purpose should be at least as interesting as its analysis, together motivate an experiment. Instead of beginning with ordinary usage, we begin with an ordinary situation. We take some prima facie plausible hypothesis about what the concept of knowledge does for us, what its role in our life might be, and then ask what a concept having that role would be like, what conditions would govern its application. Such an investigation would still have an anchorage point in the everyday concept: should it reach a result quite different from the intuitive intension, or one that yielded an extension quite different from the intuitive extension, then, barring some special and especially plausible explanation of the mismatch, the original hypothesis about the role that the concept plays in our life would of course be the first casualty. For it is not the idea to construct an imaginary concept, but to illuminate the one we actually have, though it be vague or even inconsistent; and to illuminate it by showing that a concept with the hypothesised role would have characteristics closely resembling those that it exhibits itself. But should our intuitions prove indeterminate or elastic, this type of investigation might reveal constructive ways of stretching them, and the rationale behind the stretch. With luck it might also reveal the sources of the indeterminacy or elasticity which dogged the attempts to answer, or even to ask, the first familiar question.

It can at least be said for this way of creeping up on the concept of knowledge that we are asking a question that can reasonably be expected to have an answer. One doesn't have to commit oneself to a great deal of epistemology or semantic theory, as the standard approach evidently does, to presume that there is such a thing as the point of this concept, what it does for us, the role it plays in our lives. And if this is so, one way to find out must be to form some hypothesis about it, try to work out how a concept custom-designed for that role would look, and then see to what extent it matches our everyday practice with the concept of knowledge as actually found. We may then have to revise or supplement the hypothesis from which we began, but that will hardly be surprising, and certainly no cause for instant despair.

Whilst agreeing that we may expect the concept to serve some purpose, however, we might doubt whether the consideration of its purpose will necessarily lead to anything like an analysis, or to anything that can be measured against the intuitive extension. We might doubt, in fact, whether it will necessarily lead anywhere interesting at all. Every language, an objector might reason, has a word for water. And having that word has an important purpose, namely, to make it possible to talk about water, something which every community has an obvious need to be able to talk about. But no a priori thought about that purpose will bring us any closer to an analysis of the concept of water, even if the notion of an analysis be very generously interpreted. Couldn't it just be that knowledge, like water, is common and important stuff, and that the purpose of the concept is simply to enable us to think and talk about it?

Though I would be hard put to it to argue the point, I am fairly confident that this is mistaken. Knowledge is not a given phenomenon, but something that we delineate by operating with a concept which we create in answer to certain needs, or in pursuit of certain ideals. The concept of water, on the other hand, is determined by the nature of water itself and our experience of it. But probably a better response here, at any rate a less dogmatic one, is 'the proof of the pudding': if some hypothetical but plausible purpose does issue in conditions of application showing a close fit to the intuitive extension of 'know', and does fit well with a variety of facts about the 'phenomenology' of the concept, then those who hold it to be mere coincidence may be requested to make a case for their attitude.

Another objection would be that the purpose, or purposes, of the concept of knowledge, though no doubt there are such things, are most unlikely to be anything so simple as the ones considered in this essay. The method presented here ties itself to purposes of a severely practical kind arising in what might be called a primitive situation. Suppose (and isn't it really more likely?) that the concept comes into existence in response to rather more sophisticated levels of consciousness?

With that I would initially have been inclined to agree, though I am not sure where the inclination comes from—there may just be an intellectual prejudice to the effect that everything must really be frightfully complex. Certainly there is one thing we shouldn't say in reply to this objection: that the concept under investigation is so widespread, so ancient, that it must have its origin in the most primitive requirements. What may well follow is that it must have its origin in primitive societies, but there is no guarantee whatever that primitive societies have only primitive requirements. Any society that has a well-developed language, sufficiently well developed for us to be able to say that it exercises a concept even approximately identifiable with our concept of knowledge, consists of creatures that have reached a considerable degree of mental complexity. Any number of different sorts of need may, for all we know to the contrary, follow in the wake of this complexity; so there is no a priori reason to think that we are tied by methodological principles to considering only needs of the very basic kind that I have actually tried to restrict myself to.

Again, the best response will be to treat our strategy as a hypothesis. If it doesn't work, doesn't issue in a concept having at least very close similarity to the concept we are 'explicating', then we shall have to modify the hypothesis and propose one involving rather more advanced features of human consciousness—but there is no reason to bring them in before the progress, or lack of progress, of the investigation makes it necessary to do so. To start off without them doesn't mean making the assumption that they will not in the end be needed; it is no more than good method to test the explanatory powers of the simple before resorting to the complex.

Something similar will apply to the question of what further 'needs' it will be legitimate to introduce, should that prove necessary.

We shall be looking for features of human psychology which may plausibly be supposed to be possessed by all humans, preferably ones which there is some independent reason to suppose to be possessed by all humans. To illustrate the point with an example of one which cannot without qualms be thought of in this way, we might suggest the wish to explain, in some fashion, the behaviour of one's fellows, or the wish to understand them in a way which makes them the same sort of being as oneself. (It might be thought, and has been suggested to me, that this idea could help us to see the concept of knowledge as some sort of theoretical construct, useful for explaining why other members of our community behave as they do.) But just how widespread this concern with explanation is, in particular whether it is widespread enough to fit our present bill, is very hard to say—thinking in these terms might just be a reflection of our contemporary obsession with the methods of the natural sciences. For that reason alone—there may be others—it would not be advisable to allow ourselves such a starting point before we are sure that we have exhausted the potential of far less contentious claims about the human situation, like those which I have actually tried to exploit.

We should beware of an assumption which is easy to make, but which could prove restrictive or even worse: that when we render the final account of the concept which we have constructed, this account must go comfortably into the form of a list of conditions that are individually necessary and jointly sufficient for its correct application. The standard approach sets itself the problem in this form, but whether the most illuminating response to the request for specification of the concept of knowledge has to fit it ought to be regarded as an open question, especially if we are to approach it from this different angle. In fact, I shall shortly be arguing that in trying to fit our results to it we are more likely to switch the illumination off. On the other hand, one clear fact about this matter is that the concept does lend itself at least fairly well to treatment in the standard format; and that is one of the facts which an illuminating account of it ought to illuminate, whether or not it fits that format itself. And whilst we are about it we might aspire not just to illuminate that fact, but also to cast light on the appeal of the various particular analyses that have been advocated in the literature of the topic.

I have spoken so far as if there really were something which I have called the intuitive extension of the concept of knowledge, and that the problems lay in deciding whether or not it matches the intuitive intension, and what to do about it if it doesn't. But the difficulty may go one layer deeper: is it so clear that there is such a thing as the intuitive extension at all?

To say that there is might make things sound like this: we can describe cases in terms of the facts, the subject's beliefs, the subject's relation to the facts, his mental state, and so on. Then there will be, amongst speakers of English of a reasonable level of intelligence and education who can be persuaded to give the matter their undivided attention, unanimity as to which cases exemplify knowledge; the decision, in an individual case, will depend only on the features of the case as described, and will not vary from umpire to umpire, nor with the same umpire from time to time. If that is what is implied it has to be said that it is very doubtful. There is at least some reason to think that our judgement varies with the circumstances in which we are invited to consider the case. If we come to believe that Fred has an identical twin who was in town that day, our decision that we knew that it was Fred catching the bus on the other side of the street may change. Our attitude to a lot of knowledge claims may change if we are asked to consider them with the thought of the Cartesian demon looming over us. And if it doesn't change, who is to say whether that is because we steadfastly hold to the proper application of 'know' in spite of the philosopher's attempts to deflect us, or rather because we obstinately refuse to pursue its proper application into these unaccustomed regions in spite of the philosopher's attempts to help us do so? Answers to questions like these are usually accompanied by sparks from the grinding of some philosophical axe; if we want to start from first principles we would do much better to record the fact that these 'sceptical' deliberations produce different reactions, often combined with a sense of puzzlement or irritation. Then we can take that fact as a part of the data about the life of the concept of knowledge and hope for an account which will allow us to assimilate it as it is, rather than begin by distorting it in the name of some supposedly well-defined 'extension' which the concept is arbitrarily alleged to have. Nor will we be tempted to pretend that we know where to draw a line between 'natural' and 'philosophical' consideration of knowledge-claims.

It seems, therefore, that we may be in the happy position of being able simultaneously to widen and strengthen the basis of the investigation. To widen it, because we can include amongst our *explananda* such facts as the various analyses of the concept of knowledge that philosophers have given, the fact that controversy about certain of their clauses seems difficult to resolve, the facts about the reactions to sceptical proposals like that of Descartes, and all this be it noted not instead of but as well as the 'extension' (or whatever can uncontroversially be found of it) on which the standard approach uniquely concentrates attention. And we can strengthen it, because these facts have more of the nature of an undoctored 'given' than those on which the standard approach fixates - even if it be true that all data are 'theory-laden', we have surely reduced the theoretical load.

The idea that it may be worth asking after the roots of the value of knowledge when investigating the concept has an ancient precedent. In Plato's *Meno*, Socrates wonders why we should be interested in anything beyond true belief: after all, if you believe that this is the road to Larissa, and want to go there, then acting on your belief will get you what you want just so long as it is true, so why ask any more of it? His answer is that true beliefs are even more valuable if they are stable, that is to say if we persist in holding them; and this means, so he continues, that it is advantageous to have good reasons, for then we will hold fast to the truth and not be easily lured away to falsehood.[1]

Plato's contribution here is far from negligible. But I shall not adopt it. Whether the stabilisation of true beliefs is important or not depends on which beliefs we are considering, and the circumstances of the agent—many beliefs are required for the guidance of single, 'one-off' actions under circumstances which will not recur, and once the particular occasion is past there is no obvious value at all in their persistence. (I might now need a true belief about the time; but that this belief should persist, so that tomorrow I will still know what the time was today, at the moment when I wanted to know it, may be of no interest to me whatever.) Apart from that, the possession of good reasons is not the only, nor necessarily the best, way to stabilise beliefs: effect of early upbringing, emotive ties or Humean psychological mechanisms may be just as good, and better. And apart from that again, we shall see that stability

---

[1] Plato, 97 ff. (Works are specified by the author's name and, where appropriate, a number, as listed under *References*, pp. 168–9.)

is not the only, and perhaps not even the chief, thing that we may want in a true belief.

Even if we confine ourselves to recent literature of the 'analytic' school the kind of approach I shall recommend is not without precedent. David Pears has suggested something of the kind:

It often happens, as Aristotle saw, that understanding how a thing has developed from primitive beginnings helps us to understand it in its developed form. Certainly this is true of knowledge. In this case the primitive beginning is the ability to make a discriminating response to circumstances. In the early stages the response will be a piece of overt behaviour. Later, it may be internalised, and stored for future use.[2]

This point, which Pears did not go on to press, may well be useful, but its primary use is most likely to be that of shedding light on the concept of belief, and maybe, if we add the idea of the overt behaviour, when it arrives, being in some sense successful, that of true belief. It will not in itself bring us very close to the concept of knowledge as we have it, unless an adequate account of that concept turns out (somewhat against the early odds, most of us will feel) not to need, beyond true belief, any further apparatus. So we can't rest content with Pears' remarks, though we can, and should, take his hint.

I have elsewhere[3] referred to this project as the 'practical explication of knowledge'. The notion of an explication came into currency, I believe, through Carnap. To explicate a concept was not exactly to analyse it; it was to construct a new version of it satisfying certain standards, with the proviso that to count as a new version of that concept it had to emerge with many of its principal features intact. The procedure suggested here is analogous; but it is concerned with the practical rather than (as in Carnap) the theoretical aspect of the concept. Hence the title of the earlier paper. But let it not mislead: Carnap's intentions were normative, the establishment of the concepts fit to form the rational basis of the unified science, whereas mine are the more purely theoretical ones of shedding light on the nature and origins of present practice. In that respect at least I shall follow the traditional approach.

Whilst speaking of precedents, we should notice that my project can claim membership of another tradition, one which spreads itself

---

[2] D. F. Pears.   [3] E. J. Craig (1).

altogether wider than conceptual analysis, however widely that be
conceived. I refer to the tradition of naturalism, in which thinkers
see man, his behaviour and institutions, as natural facts to be understood as the (broadly speaking causal) outcome of other natural
facts. What concepts we use, what linguistic practices are common
amongst us, these are special cases of input to the more general
naturalistic enterprise. Hume's treatment of the concept of causality
is one. Another, in a quite different area, is Hobbes account of
political and legal institutions: they are more or less adequate
attempts so to regulate the power-relationships between individuals
as to avoid the otherwise inevitable 'war of every man against every
man' and create stable circumstances in which humans, and human
society, may flourish. Robert Nozick has written—and I think there
is meant to be a note of criticism in the remark—that unlike political
philosophy epistemology has not started from a consideration of
the state of nature.[4] If that is true, and a defect, my project may
be thought of as one way to supply the lack.

Hobbes believed, of course, that normative consequences were
to be drawn: a particular kind of constitution ought to be adopted,
and in this respect other state-of-nature theorists such as Locke,
and more recently Nozick, have followed him. That is a different
matter; whether it results from my deliberations that we in any
sense ought to operate the concept of knowledge much as we do
is a question I shall not address, for unlike Hobbes's theme it is
not contentious. But it will, I believe, emerge that without it life,
whether or not brutish and nasty, would be a good deal more soli-
tary, and almost certainly shorter. Some may also wish to ask a
very different normative question: whether, if the concept of knowledge is to be developed or rendered more precise this ought to
be done in one way rather than another; clearly, there are parallels
in political theory. Again, I shall not offer an opinion; in any case,
unless we are told the purpose of such development we do well
to have no opinion to offer.

In spite of such differences, these points suggest that one might
view the whole of the following investigation in a different light:
as an adaptation to the theory of knowledge of a procedure traditionally at home in ethics and politics. I began as if our theme were
the analysis of the concept of knowledge: we were to apply a different

[4] R. Nozick, (1).

method to the same topic. Somewhat less parochially, we may think of our starting point as state-of-nature theory: we are to apply similar methods to a different object: not political, but conceptual and linguistic institutions.

Finally, before we leave the job-description for the job itself, a third connection is to be noted. 'Evolutionary Epistemology', now widely so called, is a branch-arm of the prevailing stream of naturalism. It looks at our cognitive faculties as adaptive responses to changing circumstances and changing needs for information. My investigation is akin, though it differs in two respects. First, I am not concerned, except peripherally, with any particular sensory or inferential faculties, but with our concept of knowledge in general. Secondly, I shall not treat its development diachronically, and that is not just an omission: if what I shall say is along the right lines, the core of the concept of knowledge is an outcome of certain very general facts about the human situation; so general, indeed, that one cannot imagine their changing whilst anything we can still recognise as social life persists. Given those facts, and a modicum of self-conscious awareness, the concept will appear; and for the same reasons as caused it to appear, it will then stay. Our cognitive faculties may change, and if they do then what we know will change; but that, it will be seen, is not a reason to expect the concept of knowing to change as well.

Such is the programme; we can now begin its execution. Fortunately there is a firmly fixed point to start from. Human beings need true beliefs about their environment, beliefs that can serve to guide their actions to a successful outcome. That being so, they need sources of information that will lead them to believe truths. They have 'on-board' sources, eyes and ears, powers of reasoning, which give them a primary stock of beliefs. It will be highly advantageous to them if they can also tap the primary stocks of their fellows—the tiger that Fred can see and I can't may be after me and not Fred—that is to say, if they act as informants for each other. On any issue, some informants will be better than others, more likely to supply a true belief. (Fred, who is up a tree, is more likely to tell me the truth as to the whereabouts of the tiger than Mabel, who is in the cave.) So any community may be presumed to have an interest in evaluating sources of information; and in connection with that interest certain concepts will be in use. The hypothesis I wish to try out is that the concept of knowledge is one of them. To put it briefly and roughly, the concept of knowledge is used to flag approved sources of information.

I shall not for the moment be concerned with the evaluation of what I have called 'on-board' sources. In the ordinary way we simply take it that the beliefs they mediate are true. To find oneself in possession of a belief on the question whether p pre-empts inquiry; to take a self-conscious look at one's own apparatus with the doubt in mind that it may have delivered a falsehood calls for a considerable degree of sophistication. Our investigation ought to start from the position in which we as yet have no belief about p, want a true belief about it one way or the other, and seek to get it from someone else. (I do not mean to suggest that it is ever in principle impossible for us to find out for ourselves; but in practice that will often be a hopelessly inefficient way of going about it.) Our interest in our own faculties as sound sources of information has a part to play, since under certain circumstances that interest becomes acute, for very good practical reasons; but it would not be good method to begin with it.

Consider then the position of someone seeking information on the point whether or not p. What does he want? In the first place, he wants an informant who will tell him the truth on that question. The informant, we may assume, will not in general tell him the truth unless he (the informant) holds a true belief about it. (Cases of people who, whilst not holding true beliefs, insincerely give 'information' which is in fact true, are rare; and informants who do that regularly are as good as non-existent.) So the inquirer wants an informant such that:

> Either p and he believes that p, or not-p and he believes that not-p.

This gives us a start on the analysis (or whatever we should at this stage call it) of the concept which characterises the source of information that the inquirer hopes to encounter. It is, obviously, very closely related to the first two clauses of the traditional definition of knowledge. I say 'closely related to' rather than 'identical with' only because there has been a change of perspective. The traditional analysis concentrates on the form 'X knows that p', whereas this approach directs us in the first instance to 'X knows whether p'. It is clear that the standard opening clause 'p is true' cannot feature in the analysis of the latter—we need something like the disjunctive formula given above.

The relevant part of the traditional analysis, true belief, is that which virtually all subsequent attempts to define knowledge have taken over. But before we get into the contentious area of further conditions we should pause to ask: how strong a conviction is in question here, when we speak of the informant as believing that p? Some analyses speak of certainty at this point, some of being sure. But it has been argued that being certain, or sure, or confident, is not a necessary condition for knowledge, and Colin Radford[1] has gone further and claimed that the belief condition can be dropped altogether, since cases of knowledge of p can be found in which the subject actually believes, if anything, that not-p. Does our approach have anything to say on this score? It does, though what

[1] C. Radford.

it offers is not a one-way-or-the-other decision; its contribution
is not to divide the area into black and white but rather to make
it comprehensible that this part of it should be grey.

In seeking information we are seeking to come by true beliefs;
we do not want just to have truths enunciated in our presence,
but we want to be brought to believe them, so that these beliefs,
since they are beliefs (and not mere entertainings) can guide our
actions—and guide them to success because they are true. We shall
therefore want as an informant someone who has the following
property:

   If he tells us that p, we shall thereupon believe that p.

Now because the confidence with which we believe things affects
the way we announce them, and the way we announce them affects
the likelihood that the audience will believe us, this may make it
look as if there could be some minimum level of confidence necessary
if the informant is to meet the inquirer's needs: for any lower level
he will sound so hesitant that the inquirer will probably not come
to believe what he says. To try to place a quantitative value on
that level would be silly, but it is probably not too silly to describe
it by using another vague term, and saying that if he is successfully
to induce the belief that p in his audience, he had better believe
it himself. That would make it appear that the concept we are constructing will indeed include belief as one of the conditions for a
good source of information.

But we are going too quickly—the matter is not so simple. Other
things which we believe about the informant will also play a part
in determining whether we believe what he tells us (or indeed, what
is very much the same thing, whether we select him as an informant
at all), and under certain circumstances they may well be overriding,
so that we have little tendency to believe even a very confidently
made claim, or are prepared to accept even a very diffident utterance.
Very briefly, what I have in mind is that if the informant satisfies
any condition which correlates well—as we believe—with telling
the truth about p, he will be regarded as a good source. Confidence
is only a special case of this, and not even one that we are always
prepared to use. The point will become clearer later on, after the
consideration of the further conditions—further to true belief, that
is—which we shall want the informant to meet. For the moment
we can best leave it at this: that since confidence is not essential

to performance as a source, the constructed concept will concede some ground to those accounts of knowledge which play down the belief requirement. On the other hand, it will give no support to those which want to play it down to vanishing point. In the vast majority of cases a good informant will believe the information he gives, and will give it, what is more, precisely because he believes it—the counter-examples, though perfectly genuine, are freakish. One might add that on many matters, those who hold a belief at all nearly always hold a true one, so that in these types of case possession of a belief is itself a property which correlates well with being right. These are facts about our world which cannot be without influence on our concepts. So if our hypothesis is on the right track, it is neither surprising that so many take belief to be essential to knowledge, nor that some deny it, nor that many people's intuitions leave them in the lurch at this point.

Here we see starkly a major disadvantage of the approach which takes its sole target to be the listing of logically necessary and sufficient conditions. If it can be argued that belief is not a necessary condition for knowledge, then belief will make no appearance on the final balance sheet. There is no place on it where the conceptual accountant can present belief as a major component of the constellation of thoughts which go into the practice of operating with 'know' and its cognates. He can try to talk about it, just so long as the audience is prepared to listen to such periphera, as of something which very often accompanies knowledge. But when he is asked for the real outcome of the business, the analysis, anything not strictly a necessary condition simply vanishes without trace. Of all its deep centrality nothing whatever remains—it could be as incidental as the fact that nearly all knowers are less than 150 years old.

That greater flexibility in the description of concepts is required, is hardly a new point. Wittgenstein famously wrote of family resemblance concepts, for which fixation on the format of necessary and sufficient conditions leads either to triviality or error. But we can also see, I think, why this greater flexibility is required, or at the least, why it is required in this case. We are asking not so much: when is the ascription of a certain concept correct, but rather, why is it applied? In freakish circumstances, a purpose may be achievable in unusual ways - factors which would usually frustrate it may, if other features of the situation are exceptional, do no damage, factors which are usually vital may, abnormally, be dispensable.

There is, however, an expository problem: how is this flexibility to be expressed? If we speak as if belief were not a component of knowledge we do it an injustice, if we say that it is then we risk being understood to say that it is a necessary condition. If, whenever the relation between believing and knowing crops up, we try to present the situation as it actually is, long-winded clumsiness will engulf us. I can think of nothing better than to ask the reader for a change of gear: what may look like an attempt to state necessary conditions should rather be taken as part of the description of a prototypical case, a case from which speakers and their audiences will tolerate, in the right circumstances, varying degrees of deviation. How much deviation, and under what circumstances, ought to be related to the purpose behind the formation of the concept in question. The prototypical description enshrines the features that effect realisation of the purpose when things are going on as they nearly always do.

It is important to notice that 'the way things nearly always go on' enjoys special status in this context, not just numerical advantage. We must never forget that the inquirer's situation is a practical one: he must pick out the good informant, or decide whether to make use of a volunteered statement. Now freakish cases, in which for instance he would finish up with a true belief, though the informant offer him a falsehood, or offer him a truth without believing it, are not merely rare. It is also hard for the inquirer to detect that he is in the presence of such a case—which he must do, and do confidently, if he is to make use of it; if it is possible at all it will only be because he happens to be in possession of a good deal of collateral information. To try to make a practice of detecting freakish cases would mean incurring high costs in time and energy; and successful detection would scarcely ever offer any benefit which could not be had by finding a standard informant, or investigating for oneself. In practice, therefore, it must be the standard or prototypical case at which the inquirer's strategy is directed, so that one might almost say that for practical purposes what the concept amounts to is the essential description of the prototypical case.

The words 'almost' and 'for practical purposes' are not in that sentence for nothing, however. One thing a proper account of a conceptual practice ought to be able to explain is why prima facie counter-examples to a proposed definition have (at least prima facie) the feel of being such. What is it, for instance, that gives Radford's examples some purchase? Not every account of the concept of knowledge will automatically be able to answer that question. The present suggestion does so by reference to the hypothesised purpose underlying the practice. This purpose, in conjunction with a few platitudes about the way in which human inquirers operate, generates a set of descriptive conditions; what they describe is the prototypical case in which the purpose is standardly achieved. A speaker is not taught these conditions explicitly, any more than he is explicitly taught the purpose, but when a philosopher presents them to him as logically necessary and sufficient for knowledge he is not hard to convince—after all, they apply to all the cases that readily come to his mind, and it is perfectly understandable that they should. The exotic cases, on the other hand, in which he recognises the fulfilment of the familiar purpose in the absence of one of these conditions, pull him for that reason to acknowledge them as positive instances, though very unusual ones.

Is he to go along with the pull, or is he to resist it? The practice into which he has grown up cannot be expected to help him on that point. Why should it? It has no need to legislate for cases with highly unusual features, or rather highly unusual combinations of features. No need, and in a sense it has no way to do it either. It is precisely by being *everyday* practice that everyday practice manages to impress itself upon speakers and so stay what it is. How can it help in freakish, perhaps wholly imaginary, circumstances in which some of the familiar indicators fall one way, some another? And if it could, why bother? We can always resort to expressions like 'It's almost as if he knew'.

I cannot, of course, generate the slightest appearance of a counter-example to the sufficiency of an analysis of knowledge by postulating a human subject who will be 207 years old next birthday, whom I however allow to satisfy all the conditions of the proposed analysis—by no means every unusual case is felt to be undecidable. But nothing I have said implies that it should be. For that feeling to arise the unusual features of the situation must engage with the everyday practice so as to produce some contrary pressure—to make us feel that something that matters is lacking. Not every unfamiliar circumstance need have that effect.

Certain worries call for mention at this stage, just in case they are already beginning to worry the reader. First, it is not only persons, but also for instance books and video-cassettes, that can be sources of information; but although these are sometimes said to contain knowledge, as is also a library, they are not said to know anything. Why not, if the function of 'know' is to flag good sources of true belief? One might have replied that it is because they don't have beliefs, but what we have said in the earlier parts of this section seems to imply that the present line of thought will not satisfactorily explain why that should be a reason. So there is a problem here which needs attention. Secondly, someone who has a strong motive for concealing the truth may still be said to know it. But he is of very little value as a source of information, except in those infrequent situations where the inquirer is in a position to give him an even stronger motive for revealing it. (Luigi knows exactly where Mario's body is, and how it came to be there, but there is no point at all in turning to him for information on the subject.) Thirdly, someone who both knows the truth and is keen to reveal it may be useless to others because he has no credibility with them: the boy who cried 'Wolf!' so often that no-one would believe him when the wolf really came is a cautionary example, as is Matilda of Hillaire Belloc's *Cautionary Tales*. A gap threatens to open here between the constructed concept and the concept of knowledge as we operate it, a gap wide enough to suggest that the former is too different from the latter to throw any light on it. For the moment I would just ask that we take note of these difficulties. Reacting to them involves a complication of the picture that is best postponed, since the less complicated version still has a good deal more to yield.

III

It is the third clause of the analysis, I need hardly say, which has caused all the trouble. Is it that the belief has to be based on good reasons, or that it has to have the right causal ancestry, or that it must have been acquired by a reliable method, or that it must, in Nozick's felicitous term, 'track' the fact that is its object? All these, and probably more, are on the market, some in a number of models. It has even been urged that we decline them all, and define knowledge as true belief, with no adornments. Our next question must be: does the concept that we are constructing, the one whose sole purpose is to act as a marker for approved sources of information, call for anything more than that, and if so, what?

First impressions suggest a short way with this question: no further conditions are needed. Why should we want more of a potential informant than that his views on the point at issue should be true, and at least confident enough for him to be prepared to come out with them? Then we come to hear the truth, which was what we wanted. But this overlooks a crucial point. It is not just that we are looking for an informant who will tell us the truth about p; we also have to be able to pick him out, distinguish him from others to whom we would be less well advised to listen. How is that to be done? Well, it will be easy enough to find out what he believes about p; and if we ourselves knew whether p that would suffice to tell us whether he has a true belief. But *ex hypothesi* we do not know whether p—we are in the position of inquirers, not of examiners (to borrow Bernard Williams's way of putting it); the informant is to be our means of access to that knowledge, and if we already had it, we would not be inquiring. Obviously, we have to detect the right informant without benefit of prior knowledge. So we need some detectable property–which means detectable to persons to whom it is not yet detectable whether p—which correlates well with being right about p; a property, in other words, such that if the informant possesses it he is (at least) very likely to have a true belief on that matter. The emergence of this requirement gives us, as it turns out, quite a lot to work with.

Let us at this stage set up a target for ourselves, so to speak. Nozick[1] has suggested that a knower must, besides having a true belief, satisfy two further conditions:

(i) If p were not true, he wouldn't believe that p.
(ii) If p were true (but under circumstances differing slightly from those actually obtaining) he would believe that p.

In discussing these conditions, I shall make free use of the now popular vocabulary of possible worlds (without supposing it to be anything more than a linguistic convenience); and I shall follow David Lewis[2] in saying that (i) and (ii), as counterfactual statements, are true if and only if in possible worlds close to the actual world, if p is false the subject does not believe that p, and if it is true he does believe it. I shall ask whether the practical explication we are engaged in might not lead to just these two conditions.

An immediate reaction is to ask 'Why should it?' Why should our inquirer be interested in what is the case in possible worlds? After all, he wants to be told the truth in this world, the actual world, so whence the interest in other, and merely possible, worlds, however 'close' they may be to this one? Either Nozick's 'tracking' condition is not what we are looking for, or Lewis' semantics for counterfactuals in terms of possible worlds have to be dropped. But this is too quick: there is a line of thought which shows that the inquirer cannot help being interested in the contents of possible worlds as well as those of the actual.

We have to remember that the inquirer's knowledge of the actual world is bound to be highly incomplete. It is not only that he doesn't yet know whether p; there will be all sorts of things about himself, the environment and the potential informant of which he is ignorant. There are, in other words, enormously many propositions such that he does not know whether A or not-A, whether B or not-B, and so on. So if we think of a world as defined by the totality of what is true in it, there are indefinitely many different possible worlds any one of which, so far as he knows, might be the actual world. His concern with getting the right information in the actual world

---

[1] R. Nozick, (2), pp. 172–8. See also F. Dretske.   [2] D. K. Lewis.

will therefore lead him to hope for an informant who will give him the truth about p whichever of all these possibilities is realised. Which is to say, if you like the jargon, that he wants an informant who will give him the right answer in a range of possible worlds.

Is it possible that we are not being quite rigorous enough here, and claiming more than in fact follows from the inquirer's position? The reply can be made that he is only interested in the actual world— it is just that he doesn't know, out of all those possible worlds, which one it is. What I need, he might say, is for the informant to be right in whichever of these possible worlds is the actual one; the rest can go hang—I shall have my true belief.

I doubt whether we can accept that, however. The trouble is that it leads to no strategy on the part of the inquirer. Imagine someone about to go out, and wishing to stay dry, but not knowing whether it will be raining or not, so that he faces one 'possible world' in which it will, and one in which it won't. Can he say 'I only want to keep dry in the actual world; I'm not bothered about whether I would have kept dry in whichever of those worlds turns out to be merely possible'? He can *say* it, and in a sense no doubt it is true. But if he proposes to do something about it he will either have to guess which possibility will be realised or take such action as will work in either case, even though that means planning for at least one eventuality which will turn out to have been merely possible. And the same applies to our inquirer: he must either guess which of the possible worlds he is actually in, or he must adopt a strategy which works in many merely possible worlds as well as the actual one.

Some may now have got the impression that I am about to award a prize to Professor Nozick; for haven't we said, in effect, that the search for the desired informant will naturally become a search for someone who is precisely a good 'tracker' of p, someone whose belief as to whether p is true in all close possible worlds? But I am not, for two main reasons. For one thing, Nozick does not select the right range of possible worlds, if by that we mean one that coincides with the range of interest of the inquirer. For another, Nozick's tracking condition doesn't reflect the epistemic demands that the inquirer is bound to make. I shall return to the second point later, having dealt in some detail with the first.

The first point, then, is that Nozick's range of possible worlds is not the one which will concern the inquirer; it overlaps with it, of course, but it is wider. And just this extra width causes trouble for his account, seen (in the way he surely meant it) as an attempt in traditional style to match an intension to the intuitive extension of 'know'. The practically explicated concept, on the other hand, picks the right range of possible worlds, and illuminates the reason for doing so. Here we see it scoring its first points against a prestigious attempt at an analysis of the more familiar kind.

Nozick recommends assessing his two counterfactuals by reference to what is the case in all close possible worlds. Fortunately it is not necessary for our purposes to specify exactly what 'close' means here. Roughly speaking, two worlds are said to be close to each other if they differ only slightly, distant if they differ radically, and this is accurate enough for the point I now wish to make, which is that our inquirer will not be interested in all close possible worlds, but only in those that he cannot rule out as being merely possible, or non-actual. Suppose he is considering the credentials of a potential informant whom he can see to be wearing a red shirt. There is a close possible world (and it surely is close, if the concept of closeness is to be capable of any work whatever) in which that same person is wearing a blue shirt; but since the inquirer will be perfectly satisfied that this world, although both possible and close, is not the actual world, he will have no interest in it. It is of no concern to him whether the potential informant would hold a true belief on the question at issue were he wearing a blue shirt – he already knows that he isn't.

(Here we should watch out for a point which could cause confusion. If you really thought that I would quite likely be wrong about p were I wearing a blue shirt, you would be doubtful about employing me as informant even if you could see that I am wearing a red one. But that is not be because you are taking the 'blue shirt' world into account as one in which, for your purposes, I need to be right. Rather it happens because, your beliefs about the effect that the colour of one's shirt has on capacity as an informant being what they are, for almost any value of p the belief that I wouldn't be good on p were I wearing a blue shirt will make you wonder how then I can be good on p when wearing a red one.)

If we use the expression 'open possibility' to mean a possibility which so far as the inquirer knows might be actual, we may put the point more generally in these terms: the inquirer will want the informant to be a good tracker of p in worlds that are both close and open possibilities for him, the inquirer. This will be a narrower class of possible worlds than that which Nozick uses for the assessment of his counterfactual conditions. The possibility therefore arises that Nozick's analysis will rule out some cases of (putative) knowledge where an analysis more closely tied to the situation of the inquirer would allow them. This would happen if tracking held in all the possible worlds which the inquirer will have an interest in, but failed for at least one of the wider class of possible worlds which Nozick would have us take into account.

With this thought in mind, let us look at a case which causes Nozick a good deal of trouble: the case of the Great Bank Robbery.[3] Jesse James, the reader will recall, is riding away from the scene of the crime with his scarf tied round his face just below the eyes in the approved manner. The mask slips, and a bystander, who has studied the 'wanted' posters, recognises him. The bystander now knows, surely, that it was James who robbed the bank. But Nozick has a problem: there is a possible world, and a 'close' one, in which James' mask didn't slip, or didn't slip until he was already past the bystander; and in that world the bystander wouldn't believe that James robbed the bank, although it would still be true that he did. So Nozick's condition (4)—the second of the two counterfactuals - is not satisfied, and he is threatened with having to say that the bystander doesn't know that it was James, even though the mask did slip. So his analysis looks like ruling out something which is as good a case of knowledge as one could wish for.

In the face of this problem Nozick resorts to fudging. He recalls his previous stipulation that the method by which the knowledge is acquired be held constant, so that close possible worlds in which a different method would be used to arrive at the belief that p from that used in actuality are not to figure in the assessment of the counterfactuals. And he then implies that, had James mask not slipped, the bystander would have been employing a different method, an implication which violates the distinction between the method and the evidence obtained by the use of it (as Graeme Forbes[4] has put it). A natural response to the case of the Great Bank Robbery, I believe, is that such a manœuvre ought to be unnecessary; for what would have happened if the mask had not slipped is wholly

---

[3] R. Nozick, (2), p. 193.   [4] G. Forbes, pp. 47–8.

irrelevant to the question of the bystander's knowledge. The right approach to the matter would never have let it come anywhere near the picture—then no fine and dubious distinctions would have been necessary to expunge it again. But the view from the standpoint of the inquirer has the properties we want here. Until he is satisfied that the mask did indeed slip, the sheriff will not be interested in the bystander's identification; once he is satisfied that it slipped, possible worlds in which it did not slip are deleted—they play no part, not even implicitly, in his judgement as to whether the bystander knows that it was James.

The second point about Nozick's analysis is this: What I have said so far may suggest that the difference between his 'tracking' and the conditions (in addition to true belief) which our inquirer will want to impose on his sources of information is fairly minimal: the inquirer will be happy with counterfactuals of Nozickian stamp, assessed *à la* Lewis—he will simply consider a narrower, more context-dependent, range of possible worlds. If so I apologise, because the suggestion is seriously misleading. Good tracking of the fact that p cannot be the property that the inquirer is looking for; at best it may be something that coincides with it.

I said earlier that Nozick's tracking condition does not reflect the epistemic demands that the inquirer is bound to make. The inquirer has to pick out the right informant, and no doubt it would help, even if only as a first approximation, to pick out a good tracker of the fact p. But he cannot set himself directly to pick out such a person, because the truth of a counterfactual is not epistemically primary in the sense that that would require. We don't have equipment that allows us to spot people who satisfy Nozick's counterfactuals as such. We can tell of some people that they do, and we do it not directly but by noticing something about them, perhaps the way in which they came to believe that p, which can be seen to correlate with satisfying the counterfactuals. What we ought to be looking for, at least in the first instance, is some such epistemically more accessible property.

IV

So long as we are cautious, it will do no harm to take another cue
from the current state of the literature and wonder whether Alvin
Goldman's causal theory[1] may not be what we are after. Could
the property be the causation of the belief that p by the fact that
p? Certainly there can be few better guarantees of the truth of a
belief than that it was brought about by the fact in which it is a
belief. But in spite of that, or perhaps for that very reason, it is
not very well suited to the needs of our inquirer. Sometimes, of
course, we are in a position to say that a person's belief that p is
a causal consequence of the fact that p; but under those circumstances
we already believe that p, and do not feel the need for information.
On other occasions, admittedly, there may be things about a potential informant which suggest to us that his belief on the question
whether p is caused by the facts: we saw him looking in the right
direction at the right time, for instance. And if it suggests that,
then *a fortiori* it suggests that his belief is true. But at the same
time the importance to the inquirer of the existence of the causal
connection is diminished. For his experience is that most beliefs
about the location of the cat that are formed by someone who is
looking hard at the mat turn out to be true; and this will lead him
to place confidence in their opinion, whether or not he believes
that seeing is a causal process. Human beings were good judges
of a likely source of information long before that sort of question
was ever thought of.

So there is no particular reason to think that the concept to which
the inquirer's perspective leads us will have to contain a clause about
causal connections. Like tracking, causal connections with the fact
believed are likely to be frequent correlates of the property X, but
that is all. As to what the property X may actually be, we are still
in the dark.

Points arising out of our discussion of the analyses offered by

[1] A. Goldman, (1).

Nozick and Goldman do, however, indicate an answer to that question. It is no very precise answer, but perhaps the whole point is that the property X has no very precise identity. What it suggests is simply this: X is any detectable property which has been found to correlate closely with holding a true belief as to whether p. (Some readers will think that we ought not to speak here of the particular proposition p, but rather of 'propositions of the same type as p'. They have a point, and I shall take it up later in the slightly different context of Section VII.) Any such property will give the inquirer what he needs, so long as we add one proviso: that the correlation be lawlike—an accidental correlation, one that does not support inference to a new case, will not do, since inference to the new, as yet untested case is precisely what the inquirer needs the correlation for.

In so far as such correlations are going to be causal, this lends some substance to the thought that there must be a causal connection between possessing the property X and being right on the question in hand. But this is not the same as saying that the belief in p must be a causal product of the fact that p—it does not give us the causal analysis as that is normally understood. It also chimes in with the idea that counterfactuals are in the offing—the ability to support counterfactuals has often been said to be a defining characteristic of such lawlike connections. But notice that these aren't Nozick's counterfactuals, which link p/not-p counterfactually to the belief/absence of the belief that p; rather these link the counterfactual possession of property X to the possession of the truth about p. (They say, for instance: if Fred had been looking, he would have been right about where the cat was.)

A natural way of describing the position reached would be to say that the correlation between possessing X and being right about p must be reliable. When he encounters X in a new case, his inference that its possessor will have the truth as to whether p must not lead the inquirer astray. If it can be reliable without being causal (I suspect it can), then being causal is a special case of the general principle; if it can be reliable without supporting counterfactuals (though this time I suspect it can't), then that is a special case too. But notice, once again, that this is not the same as saying that the property is that of having arrived at the belief by a reliable method, in the sense of one which (nearly) always leads to true beliefs. That property does, for obvious reasons, correlate reliably with being right; but whether it is the only property that does so is quite another question. Prima facie it seems hardly likely. After all, it might have been the case, had we been rather more scrupulous about our testimony and rather less prone to error, that the mere fact of being willing to offer an opinion correlated excellently with being right (indeed, as I said earlier, for some classes of beliefs this is pretty much the case as things are); and nobody, surely, will be prepared to stretch the concept so far that being willing to offer an opinion can be called a method of acquiring belief. The idea that there is such a correlation may be exaggerated but, as I say, it is not wholly fictitious; and at the very least it shows that it is a live question whether there are any actual states that are reliable indicators of true belief without counting by any distortion of the vocabulary as the state of having employed a certain method.

There surely are such states. If you want to know the way it will always be a good idea to ask a taxi-driver. The advice is good, because the property (which has the additional advantage of being fairly easily detected) of being a taxi-driver correlates very well with giving the right answer to that kind of question. And the property of being a taxi-driver certainly can't be identified with that of having discovered, by a reliable method, how to find one's way round the neighbourhood, although of course it is true of taxi-drivers that they have found that out by a reliable method: driving round the place for hours and hours day after day. But our inquirer doesn't need, strictly speaking, to impose any conditions on how they do it; so long as he believes that they do, and can recognise them, he can acquire the best information. It would be just the same if taxi-drivers were born that way, and never had to do anything whatever to come by their grasp of local geography.

The point can be generalised. A very large part of the art of acquiring correct information consists in being able to recognise the sort of person (or book, or whatever) that will have the right answer. So long as the inquirer is right in thinking that it has it, he will not have to concern himself with how it may have come by it, whether by a reliable method, or as a causal consequence of the relevant facts. So no such clause will appear in the concept which we are constructing—only the condition that the subject possess some detectable property that is a good indicator of true belief on the matter under discussion.

It will by now be seen that there is not going to be any more detailed answer to the query: and what property is that? There could be almost as many different answers as there are types of thing that the inquirer might want to know about. If it were not so, choosing our sources of information would be a very much simpler business than it is. But even the very general formulation that we can give is enough to enable us to link the constructed concept to the most prominent recent attempts at an analysis of the concept of knowledge. Let us begin by looking back to the counterfactual analysis of Nozick and Dretske. It adds as the further condition the two clauses:

(i) not-$p \rightarrow$ not-(S believes that p)
(ii) $S \rightarrow$ believes that p

Now in the preceding section I have in effect argued three things. First, that the inquirer must indeed be looking for an informant whose belief as to whether p satisfies such counterfactuals; that arises from the human inevitability that there are many possible worlds any of which, so far as the inquirer either knows or even believes, could be the actual world. Secondly, but in this context unimportantly, that Nozick sets the range of possible worlds across which (i) and (ii) are to be assessed too wide.

Thirdly I have also argued that, for epistemic reasons, (i) and (ii) cannot be all that the inquirer is looking for. But here the word 'all' is crucial. The epistemic point does not affect the fact that the inquirer needs an informant of whom (i) and (ii) hold—it only shows that he needs something else as well, namely something to assure him that they hold.

We can therefore see why, if my hypothesis be correct that the core of our conceptual practice using 'know' is what is constructible by taking the perspective of the inquirer, an analysis such as that of Nozick and Dretske should be felt to be close to the mark. We have not, it must be admitted, seen why it should be felt plausible to *finish* with the conditionals (i) and (ii), since the inquirer needs something further by which to detect the informant—which the truth of the counterfactuals by itself cannot enable him to do. But we can quickly convince ourselves (I shall consider this issue more slowly in Section X) that it would be easy to argue for leaving that further element out of the analysis. The informant knows, it could be said, so long as he meets the traditional requirement of true belief plus the two 'tracking' counterfactuals. The inquirer, however, needs to be able to tell that he knows, so he must exhibit some 'indicator property' X as well; but we are not obliged to take that additional X up into the analysis of knowledge.

Once we can see why the tracking analysis should appeal it is no great step to do the same for the Causal Theory. Of Hume's various 'definitions' of cause one, we may remember, was that 'if the first object had not been, the second never had existed';[2] and following that line of thought we would be lead to identify the Nozick–Dretske counterfactuals with the claim that the subject's belief that p be caused by the fact that p. Evidently these two analyses are no great distance apart.

Although the distance isn't great they are not, of course, identical. For that there are too many problems of detail about Hume's coun- terfactual definition of causation. But it is illuminating to think, bearing the literature on the concept of knowledge in mind, what some of these problems may be. One is that it makes certain processes automatically causal in nature when one would have thought that that question was at least open to discussion. If, for instance, I believe that A, infer from A that B and so come to believe that B, then the two states of my believing A and my believing B will stand to one another in the critical counterfactual relationship. Are they cause and effect? Only if inference is a causal process. Perhaps it is, but should this really be decidable in one line *ex definitione*? There is a hitch here, but, significantly, it is no problem for Gold- man's causal analysis; for Goldman simply stipulated that for the purposes of his 'causal' theory inferential processes were to count as causal.[3] Given this stipulation, the causal condition moves even closer to the third condition of Nozick and Dretske.

Goldman also said quite explicitly[4] that his analysis was aimed only at a posteriori knowledge; analysing 'know' as it applies to a priori matters was not on his agenda. With this restriction the causal condition edges still nearer to the counterfactuals. For belief in a priori truths was one of the main things holding them apart. Consider my belief that the differential of x^n is nx^{n-1}. Were it not so, I would not believe it, since I would not have seen a proof of it, nor would my teachers have told me that it was true. And

---

[2] D. Hume, p. 76.   [3] A. Goldman, (1), p. 362.   [4] Ibid., p. 357.

given that it is so, quite a lot of (small) changes could have been made to the world as it is without dislodging my belief. So the truth of the theorem and my belief that it is true satisfy the two counterfactuals. But to say that they are causally related embroils us in all manner of ontological difficulties which surely go far beyond anything we have said in merely agreeing that the counterfactuals hold: if the truth of a mathematical formula can be the cause of a belief must it not designate some kind of state of affairs, something of the sort which could enter into causal relations? And then what sort of state-of-affairs could it be, and how could its influence on our minds be a causal one? This is well-trampled ground, but fortunately there is no need for me to trample it still more. My point is simply that removing all this from consideration, as Goldman did in his early paper on the Causal Theory, helps to bring causality and tracking into near-congruence by excluding a principal area in which they may very plausibly be thought to diverge.

The next step is to see how close we now are to another popular formula, that which declares knowledge to be true belief attained by a reliable method. For some writers, indeed, there seems to be no distance at all between this formula and one or other of those we have looked at already. Ramsey[5] once defined knowledge in terms of the 'reliable method' formula, but then quickly said that what he meant by a reliable method was, or at any rate included, causal connection with the fact believed in. More recently, David Armstrong[6] made similar opening moves, and then characterised reliability in terms of satisfaction of the Nozick–Dretske tracking conditionals. But even without adopting so direct or stipulative a stance we can easily establish contact between the account in terms of reliability of method and those in terms of tracking and causal relationships.

One's first thought might be that if a certain belief satisfies the tracking conditionals, and if in addition there is such a thing as the method by which it was acquired, then that method must be a reliable method, in the sense of one which will produce the belief that p if p is the case, and will not produce it otherwise. But the first thought needs a supplement: it must be that the tracking conditionals are satisfied because the belief was acquired in that way.

---

[5] F. P. Ramsey.   [6] D. M. Armstrong, ch. 12, esp. p. 169.

Were that not so, then although the belief might be called reliable, there would be nothing particularly reliable about the method.

Now for the vast majority of human beliefs, if not indeed for all, there is such a thing as the method of acquisition. We do not just have beliefs, we come by them in specific ways. Perhaps in creatures whose mental life is much more primitive and much more instinctual than ours there are beliefs which they have not in any real sense acquired; perhaps even some very few human beliefs are like that too. But be that as it may, the vast majority of human beliefs are acquired and something, at least, can be said in description of the process by which their subject acquired them.

It does not strictly follow from this that when we trust a belief we trust it because it was acquired by such and such a method—one with a long and successful career behind it. But although that does not strictly follow it is nevertheless a fact that what convinces us, in an enormous number of cases, to place confidence in a certain belief, is a further belief about the way in which its owner—maybe another, maybe ourself—came to hold it. And even in those cases in which what did the trick was better describable as something about what the belief-holder *was* than as how he came to believe it—a teacher, perhaps, or a policeman, or a doctor—very often some view about how such people come to hold their beliefs on the appropriate subject-matter underlies and underpins our confidence in their opinions. For all such cases, therefore, the idea that what we are looking for is true belief reliably acquired will fit the bill; and since they form so large a proportion of all the cases we are likely to consider it should not be felt surprising if that formula has seemed to offer an acceptable definition of knowledge in general. For in virtually every case in which we take the counterfactual conditions to be met, we also take it that the reason why they are met lies in the nature of the method used.

It seems then that where there is tracking in consequence of the method used we have a reliable method. But the relationship between reliabilism and the tracking and causal analyses would fall apart if the converse failed, in other words if a method could be reliable without producing beliefs that satisfied the counterfactuals. That would be so if a method which generated true beliefs just in all actual cases could thereby qualify as reliable. And so long as we do not take into account the point of the concept of knowledge we might think that reliability could be so defined. But a reliable method, if it is to have any role to play in the construction of the concept of a good informant, must be a method one can actually rely on—and in Section III we have already seen how this demand brings the counterfactual property in its train.

In spite of the fact that it was alive and well in the minds of most philosophers only thirty years ago, we have not yet paid any attention to the traditional account of knowledge in terms of true belief with a reason or justification. But it should not be thought that only its recent successors are capable of the kind of treatment we have just been discussing. There are good grounds for thinking that where the minimal concept of the good informant applies, there, very nearly always, we will find true belief with a good reason as well, provided only that the notion of having a reason for a belief is not taken too strictly. Let us say that S has a reason for his belief that p if there is something else, q, such that:

(1) It is true
(2) S believes it
(3) Its truth significantly raises the likelihood that p is true
(4) S believes that (3) holds

(In including (4) I may appear to support an 'internalist' account of what it is to have a reason; but I do not wish to argue with those who would have us stop after (3). My purpose is merely tactical: since the argument I shall now give goes through if we include (4), and—as will be seen—goes through even more easily if we do not, it seems sensible to put (4) in and satisfy both the internalist and the externalist at once.)

Now it is usually true of human beings that they are prepared to offer something by way of a reason in support of any belief they hold. And 'usually' rises to 'nearly always' when we recall that (for reasons given in Section II) we will nearly always be dealing with beliefs that are held with some confidence—cases like that of Colin Radford's French Canadian will be very much the exception. Further, we are not just speaking of beliefs, but of beliefs in which S really is right and in addition to being right possesses some property which reliably goes with being right. We have seen that such beliefs are generally acquired by certain standard types of process, and human beings are normally aware of some of the more salient stages of these processes. ('Salient', admittedly, doesn't mean anything more than that they are the ones that we tend to be most aware of—but the point that follows doesn't need it to mean any more than that.)

In the case of a (true) belief acquired perceptually, for example, S will normally be aware of having had such and such visual (or other) experiences. It will be true that he has indeed had them, he will believe that he has had them, that he has had them will raise the likelihood that his belief about the state of his environment is a true one, and he will believe that it raises the likelihood. So the above conditions (1)–(4) will be met. They will also be met if we consider the standard cases of coming by beliefs about mathematics. There will be some proposition q to the effect that S has been through a process of proof or calculation that terminated in p, S will believe it, its truth will raise the likelihood that p is true, and S will believe that as well. The position is the same if we consider inferentially acquired beliefs of an a posteriori kind. Suppose I believe, truly and with some confidence, that there has been a dog in the garden. I will normally have come to this belief via the belief that there are paw-prints in the flower-bed or something similar. This something, whatever it is, will nearly always be true, since the occasions on which I will come to a true belief as the result of a false belief will be very much in the minority. The first two conditions are, therefore, satisfied. So are the others, for the truth of q (in this example: that there is a paw-print) significantly raises the likelihood of p and I will virtually always believe it to do so.

Again, suppose that I believe that there is a dog in the garden, this time because I see it. Whether we describe my reason (the proposition q of conditions (1)–(4) above) as 'my having seen the dog' or rather as 'my having had a visual experience as of a dog' is a question we can postpone—indefinitely, if we so wish. It remains true that (1) some such thing has happened, (2) in very nearly all cases I will be aware that it has happened, (3) its having happened increases the likelihood that there is a dog in the garden, and finally (4) I will be aware that it increases the likelihood that there is a dog in the garden.

If, then, 'having a reason' is captured by (1)–(4), normal human consciousness (and self-consciousness) of the processes leading to their beliefs will ensure that they have reasons for nearly all those beliefs with respect to which they are reliable informants—or which they 'know' by the lights of the constructed concept; a fortiori the same holds if 'having a reason' is sufficiently covered by (1)–(3).

Like true belief that tracks the facts, or true belief causally connected
to the facts, or true belief attained by a reliable method, true belief
with a reason is not at all far off the mark. Once again it becomes
understandable that philosophers, especially philosophers interested
in emphasising the role of rationality in human life, should have
presented the concept of knowledge in this dress.

It may be worth pausing at this stage to draw a certain parallel.
There is a similarity between some of these thoughts and a proposal
once made by H. P. Grice[7] in connection with another question.
Grice was roasting one of the old chestnuts of philosophical logic,
the relationship between 'If... then...' as it occurs in everyday
speech, and the material implication $(p \rightarrow q)$ of formal truth-
functional logic. Can one equate them? There are, of course, excellent and over-rehearsed reasons for thinking that one cannot: the
material implication comes out true, for instance, if any pair of propositions, however remote and unconnected, are substituted for p
and q, provided just that the first of them is false, or both are false,
or both true; whereas 'If I am writing about Grice, then the Moon
is about 240,000 miles from the Earth' is surely not true—at any
rate it is extremely weird and would never be said. But if they meant
the same then the second would have to be true if the first was—so
they do not mean the same. Grice undertook to show that this
well-worn argument was indecisive. He formulated certain general
principles allegedly governing all conversation, and so having
nothing in particular to do with the meaning of 'If... then...'. He
then proposed that an everyday conditional, 'If . . . then . . .', means
no more than the corresponding material conditional, and that those
features of its use which suggest otherwise do not result from its
meaning but from the operation of these general principles.

My procedure with respect to the concept of knowledge is to
some extent analogous. I allow the situation and needs of the inquirer
to generate a concept, or, as it might be better to say, a description
of a prototypical instance, roughly: 'true belief plus some property
indicative of true belief', and then suggest, in effect, that we take
this to be the core of the concept of knowledge, as Grice suggested
that we regard the material implication as the core meaning of the
expression 'If . . . then . . .'. We are then confronted with a number

---

[7] H. P. Grice. (Note that this reference offers mainly material about the general
principles governing conversation, not about the specific issue of conditionals.)

of analyses, none of them, evidently, very far from the mark; and I make no attempt to deny that there is some justification for the additions they each make to the minimal concept, much as Grice accepted that the actual use of the everyday conditional does differ from that which formal logic lays down for material implication, and that an attempt to reflect these differences in a different account of its meaning consequently has some foundation. But these very genuine differences, Grice thought, were not best described as a difference in the meaning of the expressions; and in much the same way I suggest that the differences between the 'minimal' analysis and the competing 'standard' analyses are not best seen as the outcome of the concept of knowledge. What makes them seem plausible is not the concept of knowledge, but certain very general beliefs which we all hold. These are, in particular, beliefs about the extent to which the world is a system of causally inter-related states, more specifically beliefs about the extent to which belief-states are themselves the end-product of a causal process; the belief that for nearly all human beliefs, there is such a thing as the method by which they were acquired; and the fact that human beings are usually conscious of certain stages of the processes by which they arrive at beliefs. The effect is that when the conditions laid down in the minimal concept are satisfied, it will almost always be believed that various further conditions are satisfied too: in particular, those of Nozick and Dretske, those of Goldman's causal theory, those of the reliabilist in so far as they genuinely differ from these; and finally (to reverse the chronology) those of the traditional analysis of knowledge as true belief with a reason.

V

We now need to pick up a hint from the last section, and take a closer look at a distinction which I have so far smudged over, though it is an important one. There are informants, and there are sources of information. Or, to arrange the terminology differently, among the various sources of information there are on the one hand informants who give information; and on the other there are states of affairs, some of which involve states of human beings and their behaviour, which have evidential value: information can be gleaned from them. Roughly, the distinction is that between a person's telling me something and my being able to tell something from observation of him. Of course, in this evidential sense it is far from being only persons that are sources of information. A tree is a source of information on its age, since one can tell its age by counting the growth-rings; in fact, anything is a source of information on a great variety of matters—given a suitably equipped observer who knows which inferences to draw.

In general terms it can be said that the concept of knowledge, as we operate it in everyday practice, is tied to informants rather than to sources of information in the sense just (approximately) characterised. We don't speak, even metaphorically, of a tree as knowing how old it is; and if Fred enters dripping wet, although he may well know that it is raining, we don't say that he knows it just because we can tell it by looking at him.

Just to draw this distinction isn't enough; we need some idea as to why it should have been felt worth drawing, otherwise we shall find that our 'practical explication' leaves us still a very long way from the concept of knowledge as we find it in use. Why bother to build into the vocabulary a distinction, amongst sources of information, between 'informants' who 'know' on the one hand and other sources which do not know on the other? The answer cannot lie in the distinction between agents and non-agents, for the second example of the previous paragraph proves that an agent can be a source of information in both ways; indeed an agent's actions can be sources of information in both ways, as a little further thought shows. And even if this were not so, we would still be left wondering why, if what we are after is true belief, we should attach importance to the distinction between getting it from something that acts and getting it from something that doesn't. More promising are two other thoughts, namely (i) the convenience of an informant as opposed to a 'mere' source of information, and (ii) the special psychology of team-work in a community, something which is involved in the use of informants but not in the use of sources of information. The point about convenience is that anyone who understands both the question (a test which the inquirer can hardly fail) and the language he speaks or gestures he uses can get information from an informant, whereas getting it from a 'source of information' will often call for various degrees of more specialised knowledge, perhaps for a special ability to evaluate evidence. In comparison with (i), (ii) is more questionable, and far harder to pin down; for this reason it would be awkward if one had to rest—as we fortunately do not— the whole case for the importance of the informant/source of information distinction upon it. But it is still worth mentioning. What I have in mind is the special flavour of situations in which human beings treat each other as subjects with a common purpose, rather than as objects from which services, in this case true belief, can be extracted.[1]

It isn't all a matter of 'special flavour', a little additional cosiness. There is another, and this time much less elusive, factor: an informant is a co-operating member of our species. That means that he can often empathise with the inquirer, and react not just to the question but to the presumed purpose of asking it, so giving the inquirer useful information that he didn't know he had need of. 'Where's the bus stop', he asks, and is told not just 'Fifty yards down there on the right', but in addition: 'And that's the last bus just turning into the road.' Mere sources of information, on the other hand, though they may often be extremely useful, are never actively helpful. How could they be? They don't know what the inquirer is up to.

Once we have this distinction in view a number of other lines of thought open up. I should like to begin with this one: that if

---

[1] In this connection see A. Ross.

knowing has to do with being an informant as opposed to just being a source of information, this could do something to explain our reluctance (which does not seem to amount to complete refusal) to regard someone who does not believe that p as knowing that p.

Let us begin with a case in which we can use as a source of information as to whether p someone who would certainly not be said to know whether p. Fred is, as I am aware, systematically wrong about what day of the week it is: he is always a day behind. Now I can certainly find out which day it is by asking him: if he says Thursday, I can rely on its being Friday, and so on. But Fred neither knows what day it is, nor is he a good informant; for he does not tell us, or even believe, that it is Friday. Likewise, if there are two identical twins well known to me, Judy and Trudy, and Fred knows one but is not even aware of the other's existence, then I may find out that Judy is in town from Fred's telling me that he has just seen Trudy—for I happen to know that Trudy is somewhere else, so it must have been Judy that Fred saw.

Now we may move to the case in which the 'informant'—if rightly so called—actually tells us the truth: Radford's French Canadian, Jean. Jean comes out with the right answers to questions about British history, and someone who knows the background to this surprising fact can certainly find out about British history by accepting what Jean says. Notice that he does accept what he says; it is not that he infers that p from Jean's assertion that q, as in the examples of the previous paragraph. Nevertheless, that does not feel wholly to settle the question whether he is treating Jean as informant, or only as source of information. One can understand the hesitation. The situation is extremely like the familiar one in which we ask a straight question and receive a straight and reliably correct answer. 'Tell me', says the interrogator, 'when did Elizabeth I die?' And Jean says '1603'. But something is missing: does Jean actually tell us these things, or does he just come out with numbers in response to our questions? Or something lying mistily half way between? So Radford's example does not (for reasons further to those mentioned in Section II) absolutely force acceptance of the view that there can be knowledge without belief. For an opponent could say that where there is no belief there is no genuine communication or 'telling', and argue that we should therefore assimilate Jean's case to one in which a piece of behaviour serves as an excellent source of information (that is, a very useful piece of evidence) to any audience with the needful background knowledge. For this view of the matter the fact that the behavioural evidence in question happens to be a verbal expression of the right answer is inessential and confusing.

Radford prefers a different assimilation: crucial for him is the undoubted resemblance to the standard and familiar situation. 'Prefers' may well be the operative word. Neither side has said anything false. Both similarities exist, both are striking. And they are not quantifiable, so is it any wonder if we are torn between them?

These thoughts can also throw light on certain cases mentioned earlier[2] as prima facie difficulties for our basic thesis: books and the like, excellent sources of information, but never, even in the spirit of metaphor, said to know anything. In terms of the distinction we are considering, they are regarded not as informants but as sources of information. Not that specialist knowledge of any kind is required to unravel their secrets—a large part of their point is to provide a perspicuous source, accessible to anyone with a command of the language they use. But they have none of the psychology of the prototypical informant: they have no beliefs, they do not act, they are not felt to co-operate with us, and they cannot empathise with us so as to anticipate our purposes. Besides, they have a special place amongst sources of information: they are the evidence laid down by creatures that *are* prototypical informants precisely as the most perspicuous vehicle of their information. The most natural thing for us to assimilate them to is the voice of a speaker, something which, if I may be allowed a modest phenomenological flourish, we 'hear straight through' to the person speaking. I would not deny that it is possible, in some contexts even legitimate, to think of them as some kind of evidence; but that is a highly unnatural posture of mind which we can achieve only with sophisticated theoretical effort.

The distinction between informant and source of information also has a role to play in the discussion of another area of the topic; and it will turn out later that its effect in this area is important. Some writers have drawn attention to what they call a 'comparative' aspect of the concept of knowledge: a person might be said to know that a piece of music was by Mozart, in circumstances where the

[2] Above, Section II, last para.

alternative was that it was by Bartok, but not to know if circumstances were such that the alternatives included Hadyn. Such examples, if genuine, cannot help but cause difficulties for an account of knowledge which sees it as a relationship between the subject and the fact that the piece is by Mozart, for it must be explained how this relationship comes to be altered by the circumstance that if it were not by Mozart, it would be by Bartok (those being the only two pieces on the radio at the moment). But if we think of the inquirer looking for a good source of information, we see that these 'comparative' considerations can easily find a place. For the inquirer may already have reached a stage at which the alternatives, for him, have been reduced to just those two (for he has checked with the published programme). If he has, then his standards for an informant will naturally be much less demanding than if he has not. (And someone who has not already excluded the possibility that all our experience could be the work of Descartes' demon might set his standards impossibly high.)

The inquirer-based conception therefore seems to fit comparativism like a glove. One might be inclined to think that it fits it no better than does the tracking analysis, which is of course perfectly placed to bring in considerations about what would have happened had the piece not been by Mozart. That may be, but how well placed is it to bring in the point, vital to the example, that if the music had not been by Mozart it would have been by Bartok? What is so 'close' about the world in which Bartok was to be heard? Granted that the world in which the radio is tuned to the other channel isn't far away, but neither, so far as we can see, is a world in which the channel that was in fact playing Mozart is playing Haydn—perhaps the compiler of programmes tossed a coin, heads Mozart tails Haydn. And if that world were adjudged close, the claim that the subject knows that the piece was by Mozart might well fall, whereas it would stand if we considered only the Bartok-world. We can see far more readily, I believe, why the Bartok-possibility takes preference over the Haydn if we allow these preferences to flow from the state of mind of an inquirer who has already satisfied himself that Mozart and Bartok (but not Haydn) are the relevant alternatives.

Unfortunately, however, there is a strong suspicion that comparativism is spurious, and that the concept of knowledge presents no such phenomena as those we are trying to explain. At best, its status is much like that of the beliefless knowledge of Radford's Jean, as I shall now argue. Let us first distinguish two situations:

(A) The inquirer, knowing that whatever was on the radio must either have been Mozart or Bartok, selects an informant who will give the right answer when the question is put to him as a disjunction of those two possibilities.

(B) The inquirer puts the question in the open form ('Which composer wrote the music you were listening to this morning?'), receives the answer 'Mozart' and takes that to be the right answer. Here again we need to distinguish two possibilities:

(i) He believes his informant to be very good at distinguishing Mozart from any other composer.

(ii) He believes that his informant would at any rate not say that it was by Mozart had it been by Bartok. (Though might had it been Haydn, or early Beethoven, or C. P. E. Bach.)

Now surely there is at most one of these cases in which we should feel decisively (given a moment's thought) that the informant knew that the piece was by Mozart, and that is (B)(i). For on reflection we immediately see that nothing is needed for (A) except that the informant be able to tell, of anything that is *de facto* by Mozart, that it was not written by Bartok; strictly speaking no more than that is needed for (B)(ii) either, though one would have to accept an element of coincidence, in that the informant has correctly picked Mozart out of the bunch of composers whom he might just as well have chosen on hearing that music. What is happening here, in fact, is that the inquirer is taking the informant's utterance, putting it together with what he (the inquirer) knows about the situation (including the capacities of the informant), and deducing the truth on the question he is interested in. He is using the so-called informant's utterance as a piece of evidence, not as a piece of information—this is obscured by the fact that the same words in the mouth of a different person (the informant of (B)(i), for instance) would be used as information.

Notable about (B)(i), of course, is the fact that the inquirer's special knowledge is playing no part. It might have done so if the informant had said that the piece was by Bartok—for the specification of case (B)(i) does not guarantee that this informant can tell Bartok's music from that of every other composer, only that he can tell it from Mozart's. And if there is a variety of other composers whom he cannot reliably tell from Bartok we would resist the idea that he

knew that this music was by Bartok even though he got the answer
right, and at the same time enabled the inquirer to conclude confidently that it was indeed Bartok he had been listening to. The ascription of knowledge, in other words, seems to stop just where specific
knowledge on the part of the inquirer is needed if he is to make
use of the 'informant'; and this coincides with the distinction we
intuitively make between using someone as an informant and using
their behaviour (including their utterances) as a source of information, or more precisely as evidence. Notice that in case B(ii) our
inquirer would have got the information he wanted (that the music
was by Mozart) had he been told that the music was by Haydn—so
long as he believed that the 'informant' would not at any rate take
Bartok's music for Haydn's. Once we have the crucial distinction
in mind we see that the informant is not clearly functioning as an
informant at all.

Ascriptions of knowledge may, as we shall later see, be in a certain
sense relativised to an inquirer's concerns. But they are not relativised to any special knowledge of the circumstances surrounding
his inquiry.

Alvin Goldman[3] has drawn attention to facts about the phenomenology of 'know' which are surely germane here. Henry, driving
in the countryside, sees a barn, and we may imagine circumstances
to be such that we unhesitatingly agree that he knows that that
is what it is. (Circumstances are, in other words, pretty much normal; and nobody has recently been putting any of the sceptic's
favourite possibilities into our heads.) Goldman now asks us to suppose that we hear that, unknown to Henry, this stretch of country
is full of papier mâché barn-façades, very plausible ones, which
Henry would not be able to distinguish from a real barn given the
amount of attention he can spare from the driving seat. Now do
we think he knows that this barn (this one really is) is a barn?
Most of us will think not, in spite of his being, in fact, right in
this case. Had he been 2 miles further down the road, let us say,
he would have looked out of the window, unhesitatingly identified
a barn, and been wrong.

Now vary the conditions. Suppose that there is only one such
fake barn, but that it is very close to the barn that Henry has (correctly) identified—perhaps the very next one down the road is the

<hr>

[3] A. Goldman, (2), esp. Section I.

one that will catch him out. Decide how you feel, then try another variation: there is only one such fake barn, and it is nowhere near Henry's route. Or there was once such a 'barn', but it was destroyed 5 years ago. Or there never was such a barn, but someone once thought of making one and then decided not to bother. Or it is just that it is a physical possibility to make one.

My own reaction here (and I take it that it will be widely shared, or that I will quickly be notified if it isn't) is that at the beginning of the sequence I am reluctant to say that Henry knows that he is seeing a barn, but that thereafter my reluctance falls off sharply. How does this compare with the reactions of an inquirer weighing Henry up as a possible informant?

We need to be very careful here as to exactly what the inquirer knows at the outset. If he just knows that the fake barn is very close to Henry, and here is Henry now announcing a barn, then obviously he will be unwilling to use Henry as an informant, much as we are unwilling to allow that he knows. But then comes an anomaly. If the inquirer knows all that and a little bit more, namely that the fake barn is not, as a matter of fact, the thing that Henry is now looking at, won't he then be happy to rely on Henry to tell him whether or not the thing he is looking at is a barn? Surely he will, so long as he can eliminate the possibility that it is the fake barn—everything else around here Henry can perfectly well distinguish from a barn. Yet the knowledge that it isn't the fake barn that Henry is looking at doesn't increase our willingness to say that he knows that the thing he is looking at really is a barn. There seems to be a mismatch here between our intuitive use of the concept of knowledge and the inquirer's view of the adequacy of an informant—so the discrepancy has to be explained.

We can explain it by calling once again on the distinction between the informer and the source of information. Henry ceased to be a desirable informant when we heard that there was, close to him, a fake barn-façade which he would not manage to distinguish from a real one. Receiving the further news that whatever Henry was looking at when he announced a barn was at any rate not the said barn-façade, and being satisfied that there was nothing else that he would mistake for a barn, we could make use of him after all. But notice that 'make use of' seems to be about the right way of putting it: it is only because of some special piece of knowledge which our imaginary inquirer happens to have (and Henry doesn't) that he

can take Henry's affirmation as a basis for the belief that there is
a barn there. Because what he comes to believe is identical with
what Henry told him there is some temptation to think that Henry
is here informing him of the barn. But in view of the way in which
the inquirer uses his special ancilliary information, and wouldn't
form a belief without it, the case is just as easily assimilated to that
in which Henry announces a barn and the inquirer, aware that at
any rate there is no barn there, infers that it was the barn-façade.

Tentatively, we may make a more general point. Clear is at any
rate this: the fact that whether the object he sees were a barn or
a barn-façade Henry would say that he saw a barn, is something
that will not in practice not bother our inquirer. More accurately:
it will not bother him unless he assigns a significantly high probability to the alternative that it is a façade. This, I conjecture, is
what is at work on us in the series of situations just envisaged.
The mere logical possibility of a indistinguishable object gives no
boost to the thought that it is the fake that Henry is looking at,
the physical possibility (by itself) doesn't do so either; even the
knowledge that someone once conceived the intention of making
one has very little effect. If we are told that they actually did it,
then something stirs; and if we are told that they did it near here
the matter begins to get serious. If, finally, we hear that there are
several of the things along this very stretch of road, then we cease
to look to Henry to tell us where the (true) barns are. And our
judgement as to whether Henry knows that it is a barn (given that
in fact it is) tends to keep step with this progression: at the beginning
he does, at the end he doesn't, in between we waver in varying
degrees.

Now, in one of the cases in which the likelihood that this is the
barn-facade seems to have grown large enough to matter, imagine
our inquirer to be in possession of additional information which
lowers that likelihood again. Our trouble was at first that he may
still use Henry as an informant, but we then saw that this is not
really what he is doing: he is using Henry in conjunction with his
own additional information to arrive at a belief, and so Henry is
serving him as a source of information. When we asked earlier what
gave us a practical interest in the distinction between informant and
source of information, a central component of our answer was that
some routes to reliable belief were open only to particular inquirers,
those specially equipped with background information and

VI

A general problem seems to arise with all definitions or analyses of the concept of knowledge. Whatever conditions are proposed, it seems possible to arrange for them to be fulfilled 'by accident'. Gettier's examples, and the numerous subsequent variants on them, do this for the analyses in terms of having good reason; examples of deviant causal chains do it for an analysis in causal terms; examples such as those adduced by McGinn[1] do it for the counterfactual analysis of Dretske and Nozick.

In this section I should like to investigate two questions, of which the first is this: why is it that when we deem fulfilment of the conditions to be accidental we withhold the ascription of knowledge? It might be answered simply by saying that the concept of knowledge requires the truth of the belief to be non-accidental. So it does, but the answer is deficient in at least two ways. In the first place, it makes it sound as if the point were just that the traditional conditions (1) and (2) can be satisfied 'by accident', that the concept will not tolerate this and therefore requires a third condition. Whereas the point is more: when we add a third condition it turns out possible to think of ways of fulfilling all three such that the existence of the true belief, the fulfilment of (1) and (2), still strikes us as accidental in spite of the fulfilment of (3)—and when that happens we deny that there is knowledge.

The minimal answer is deficient in a second and deeper way. It tells us nothing about why the concept of knowledge should be resistant to such accidental fulfilment; most concepts can perfectly well be applicable by accident or coincidence without on that account being any the less applicable. A bachelor, Quine has taught us, is an unmarried man. Anything that satisfies those two conditions is a bachelor, anything that is both a fox and female is a vixen. Nobody is worried by the question whether, relative to the fact of a given person's being unmarried, it is 'accidental' that he is male,

---

[1] C. McGinn, this passage pp. 532–3—see below, p. 58, n. 4.

or whether relative to a given animal's being female, it is accidental that it is a fox. In cases like these there is no order of priority amongst the conditions, no requirement that a particular one of them should somehow connect with the fulfilment of the others and render it 'non-accidental'.

Nor—one might think of this as a third defect—does the minimal answer tell us what we are to understand by 'accident' in this context. Too much is left unspecified, too much unexplained; the hope is that our 'practical explication' will help illuminate the fact that the concept has this feature, whilst at the same time suggesting more precisely just what the feature is.

What the inquirer wanted, we recall, was someone who believes the truth about p, and has some detectable property X, possession of which correlates well with being right about p, that can guide the inquirer in his choice of informant. Remember also that he wants there to be a more than merely *de facto* correlation between X and the truth of the belief, for it must be legitimate for him to rely on the correlation on this (as yet untested) occasion. Now suppose we are satisfied, for given X and p, that the right sort of correlation holds; we rely on it, and are given what we later find out to have been the right answer. But we also find out that features normally needed to make the connection reliable were missing. As I have said in another, related, case, what makes the connection reliable was not, we discover, operative here. We knew things about the informant which correlated well with being right as to whether p. We now discover further facts and have to accept that his chances of being right, if all *that* was the case, were very much lower than we were previously lead to believe.

In what ways could the correlation between possessing X and being right as to whether p be unsatisfactory to an inquirer seeking a good informant? We may start at the position in which the inquirer believes that this correlation has held (at least nearly always) in the past. The first problem could be that he believes that this (almost) universal generalisation is only accidentally true, and so of a kind that does not support an inference to the case he is at present considering.

Let us suppose that point to be out of the way, so that the correlation is taken to be lawlike—it rests on something or other which would normally permit the inquirer to extend it to the new case. Now what else could be wrong with it? Here are some suggestions:

1. It is a correlation that you wouldn't know about unless you yourself knew, in this instance, whether p.

2. It is a correlation that you wouldn't know about unless you had a great deal of specialised knowledge about this particular instance.

The first of these we can forget—under those circumstances you would not be inquiring. The second might be the case if in Bernard Williams' example,[2] for instance, you knew that the only way the chairman was at all likely to come by the belief that the accountant is depressed was via the causal route actually traversed. Another way of putting this might be to say that the property in question, X, would be something immensely complex, so that only someone with minute knowledge of this particular chairman, this accountant, and this firm's affairs, could tell that he had it. He would have to be in a position to argue: the chairman could only come to believe that the accountant is depressed if he is depressed himself—the only thing that could depress him would be the belief that the firm is in difficulties—the only thing that could make him think that the firm is in difficulties would be his hearing a pessimistic report from the accountant—the only thing that could cause the accountant to give such a report would be his (the accountant's) depression. Then he could argue that if the chairman believed that the accountant was depressed there was a very high probability that the accountant was depressed. (You might then say that there was a whole lot more knowledge necessary, to ensure that if the chairman believed that the accountant wasn't depressed there was a very high probability that he wasn't.) It is clear that none of these 'The only thing that . . .' clauses would be believed except by someone with minute and intimate knowledge of the whole situation. Furthermore, someone with that much knowledge would virtually never believe them, since they would virtually never all be true, even if any of them were. In other words, this route to the conviction that the chairman was a good informant on whether the accountant was depressed would virtually never be open, for any practical purposes one may confidently say never.

[2] B. A. O. Williams, (1), p. 7.

Another possibility:

3. There is something about the present case which makes the continuation of the correlation accidental in this instance.

Notice here, for clarity, that we must carefully distinguish between the circumstance of the (near) universality of the correlation having been accidental in the past—in which case no inference to the present case would be warranted—and its being accidental in the present case in spite of not having been accidental in the past. (This might be so if some of the essential conditions which made it happen in the past have been removed, but it happens nevertheless, and indeed this would be just the structure of the standard type of Gettier-example.[3])

We should ask, what is wrong with the correlation's being accidental in this instance, if *de facto* it holds? After all, the inquirer will take it to hold, in virtue of its having held up to now, and since it does hold in the present case (no matter how that comes about) he is led to pick an informant who will in fact tell him the truth. So he gets what he wanted; is there any reason to be dissatisfied?

One reply is this: that although in one sense he gets what he wanted, that is the truth as to whether *p*, there is a good deal that he would have liked to get with it—and doesn't. He would have liked, for instance, the assurance that he could use that informant again on similar questions; but quite the contrary, he is actually warned against it, and must now begin to look elsewhere. This reply, however, is for two reasons not sufficient. First, it leaves one wondering why the fact that our inquirer did not get something else should so cloud the fact that he did get sound information about *p*. Of course, if it were clear that inquirers were never looking for anything so specific as information, on that occasion, as to whether *p*, but always for informants who were right in general on that kind of question, then it would be clear what they felt to be missing. But far from being clear, it doesn't even sound likely. It may be (we shall shortly consider the question more carefully) that being right on one issue nearly always goes along with being trustworthy on a range of others, but why that should stop someone counting as a good informant on the single issue in circumstances in which that property doesn't draw the more general reliability along with it still awaits explanation.

I mean that to be taken at face value, not as a rhetorical denial

[3] E. Gettier.

that an explanation can be found. But whether it can be found or not, our reply faces the more immediate charge that it relies on a falsehood. The cases in which it turns out to have been accidental that the chosen informant gave the right information are not by any means all of them such as to cast doubts on his trustworthiness on like questions on other occasions. Having been the luckless fall guy in a Gettier case, for instance, doesn't leave one stripped of all credit; after all, Smith proceeded according to the best canons of evidence and reasoning. Gettier cases draw attention to the fact that even very good reasons indeed can let you down; but if that be allowed to tell against Smith's credentials then it tells against everybody else's. Of course, it doesn't do either. The correlation between having excellent reasons and being right is still what it always was: fallible, but virtually unfailing.

Of course, there are cases of being right by accident which reveal in their detail some misuse of the evidence, incapacity to gather it, or insensitivity to important distinctions within it; and these do blacken the character of the potential informant and make him for the future in-, or at any rate less, eligible. But that all cases of being right by accident are like this simply cannot be maintained; so it cannot explain our response to accidental true belief in general, and not to Gettier-type cases in particular.

However, the discovery that the correlation between possessing the property X and being right about p was in this instance accidental will have a characteristic effect on one's attitude to the very instance in question, quite apart from what it does to one's readiness to employ that informant on other, related, issues, or on the same issue on other occasions. It produces that retrospective feeling of having run a risk, of having done something that one would not have done had one just been a little better informed at the time, rather like finding that the person who has just driven you 50 miles down a busy motorway without incident hasn't passed the driving test. Believing in a disjunction (as Smith did in Gettier's second case) on the grounds of a false belief in the first disjunct may sometimes come out right. But it can hardly be recommended as a policy. Those writers[4] who, faced with Gettier's counter-examples, sought to modify the 'Justified true belief' analysis by adding a 'no false lemma' clause certainly had a substantial point on their side: the

---

[4] Here I am thinking in particular of Keith Lehrer and Gilbert Harman.

best of reasoning only preserves truth; it has no capacity of itself to regenerate it once lost. If a train of reasoning passes through or in any way relies on a falsehood it can only be luck if it culminates in a true conclusion.

It may be possible to exploit these considerations about being accidentally right to explain a prominent feature of the literature, namely that whatever conditions (call them X) are proposed to supplement (1) p and (2) S believes that p, it seems possible to find an example in which the connection between S's satisfying X and his being right as to whether p is accidental, and this invariably strikes us as a counter-example to the proposal that knowledge be defined as (1)&(2)&X—these conditions, whether necessary or not, turn out to be insufficient. Now if we are looking for an X such that possession of X gives a high probability of being right as to p, then it is only to be expected that all analyses that specify the X will turn out to be defeasible, for this is just what would happen to any attempt to lay down specific necessary and sufficient conditions for the practically explicated concept of the good informant. The thought is that

S has X entails: It is highly probable that S is right about p, which has the form

E entails: It is highly probable that C

But we know from consideration of the logic of probability statements that unless E actually entails C itself, it is invariably possible to find something else, D, which is both compatible with E and such that

(E and D) does not entail: it is highly probable that C

thereby showing that E did not entail it either. This, I suggest, is what lies behind the discovery that every analysis of 'S knows that p' turns out to be defeasible by counterexample. The logic of conditionals of the form

If E, then probability of $C = n$

is not, as the jargon goes, monotonic: only for the special case in which $n = 1$ can we add premises to the antecedent and still rely on the consequent.

Let me try putting this another way. Offered as sufficient conditions for S knows whether p are:

S is right as to p, and
S has X

We have seen that our practically explicated concept will have similar structure. Of first importance will be that

(S has X) gives high probability to (S is right as to whether p)

For if S has X and it is not highly probable that he is right about p then the fact of his possessing X (and merely *de facto* being right about p) will not mean that he satisfies the constructed concept—these conditions will not be sufficient. An inquirer (who does not of course know that he is right about p) should not make use of him as an informant on the basis of his possession of X.

Now imagine someone to have proposed a specific value for X. Note that having X must not entail that S is right as to whether p—we have seen long ago that that makes X far too strong a condition to be necessary. But it seems that having X must entail that it is very probable that S is right about p, otherwise it would be logically possible that S has X but that still it is not probable that he is right as to whether p, and in that case he won't satisfy the constructed concept, so the conditions proposed are after all not sufficient ones.

But it is well known that probability statements have a certain property of defeasibility which makes it impossible to find evidential statements E which, whilst not entailing a conclusion C, nevertheless do entail that C is highly probable. It seems always possible to find something further, D, which is compatible with E, and such that although on the basis of E alone one would regard C as highly probable, on the basis of (E & D) one would not.

An example: when we hear that Dancing Brave has won his last five races against top-class opposition and was clearly in the best of health at exercise yesterday, we regard it as very probable that he will win again this afternoon. If we add to that evidence the further statement that Big Nig was seen in his stable this morning tipping some white powder into his drinking-water, we cease to regard a win this afternoon as likely. If we learn that the white powder was only glucose we change back. If we hear that on his way out Big Nig passed a bundle of bank notes to the prospective jockey we lower the probability again, and so on.

What this suggests is the following: there is not going to be any property X such that possession of it by S absolutely has to be regarded as conferring high probability on S's being right about p, no matter what else we may know about S and his circumstances; there will always be something else which we could come to believe (call it Y), such that (X and Y) doesn't lend much probability to 'S is right as to whether p'. Examples of this kind will always be available to show that the proposed analysis does not offer sufficient conditions. The constructed concept thus turns out to have a feature which the concept of knowledge, to judge by the recent course of the debate, seems to have as well.

It would be premature at this stage to conclude that no set of conditions can be sufficient for knowledge, that strictly *all* attempts to state sufficient conditions must be 'Gettierisable'. Any condition, for instance, which included the blanket proviso that there was to be no true proposition having the properties of our D (or Y) would seem to be immune to the above line of reasoning. We shall return to the question in Section IX. For the moment we might explore another path, and see if our constructed concept will resemble the concept of knowledge in respect of what Simon Blackburn[5] has called the Mirv/Pirv principle. He stated it as follows:

If two subjects each believe truly that p, then one cannot know, when the other does not, unless the former is in a position with at least as much IRV as the latter.

IRV is 'information receiver value'; it refers to the subject's capacity to receive evidence and to think about it (if necessary) so as reach sound beliefs. Suppose we equate this (realising however that the equation is not completely obvious) to reaching beliefs with a high probability of truth. Since our inquirer, in looking for a good informant, is looking for someone whose opinion on the matter in hand has a high probability of truth, it is almost trivially true that he will operate the Mirv/Pirv principle. For at whatever level he sets the probability that he requires if he is to take someone as an informant, obviously it cannot arise that he will take Fred when he will not take Mabel unless he rates Fred's probability higher than Mabel's. If Mabel is below the line Fred cannot be above it unless his probability of being right is higher than hers; in other words, it cannot be right to accept Pirv when you will not accept Mirv.

[5] S. W. Blackburn.

That point does not of course touch the question how we assign these comparative probabilities in the first place, but the example which follows in Blackburn's paper gives some indication. There Mirv and Pirv have the same evidence, but crucial to what they are going to make of the evidence is a certain question about the likely behaviour of a professor—and on this point Mirv has the true belief and Pirv the false one. On the basis of this description of the situation we give Mirv the better chance, for we quite reasonably take it that someone who, in reasoning, is operating with true beliefs has a better chance of success than someone who is at some point relying on a falsehood. What is at work here, in other words, is the very same principle as governs the response to Gettier's examples. As with the various competing analyses, here too our approach unifies prima facie distinct features of the literature.

VII

The analysis of the concept of knowledge widely known as 'Reliabilism' can take a number of forms. Once it has been said that knowledge is true belief acquired by a reliable method the question arises what the method has to be reliable for, and a variety of answers are in theory possible:

(*a*) For producing a true belief as to whether *p* in precisely those circumstances;

(*b*) For producing a true belief as to whether *p* in circumstances much like those obtaining;

(*c*) For producing a true belief as to whether *p* in pretty well all circumstances likely enough to be worth considering,

(*d*) For producing a true belief as to whether *p* in all possible circumstances.

All of these relate just to a particular proposition, *p*, and increase in strength by stepping up the range of circumstances across which the method is to work. We might also increase strength in another dimension by requiring that the method work not just for the proposition *p* but for all propositions relevantly like *p*. Here of course the stringency of the requirement rises as we adjust the notion of relevant likeness so that a larger and larger class of propositions becomes involved.

I do not for the moment want to say anything about attempts to decide where to stop on the scale from (*a*) to (*d*); material relevant to that question will occur elsewhere in this essay. It is debatable, and debated, where on the second of these dimensions is the proper resting place for an account of knowledge; let us turn our attention to this debate. McGinn, for instance,[1] objects to Nozick's analysis that it is concerned with reliability only with respect to the one proposition *p*, and himself opts for reliability across a rather more inclusive class. Yet there are some cases—such as that of someone

---

[1] C. McGinn, p. 536.

who knows his own name but is no good at finding out anyone else's—which suggest that the 'single proposition' analysis may have something to be said for it. Can the technique of practical explication be used to throw any light on the matter?

We can arrive at much the same question from another direction, one highly pertinent to the approach I am recommending. McGinn makes a suggestion[2] about the pragmatic value of the concept of knowledge. Knowing that p, according to his view, involves being good at getting true beliefs on a range of associated questions, so 'if we know that S knows that p we can infer . . . a number of truths about the world given information about S's other (relevant) beliefs'. Now I attempt to construct the concept by considering the situation of someone who is looking for the truth on the sole question whether p—my inquirer as presented is not looking for the truth on a range of issues similar to whether p.

This raises the question: ought I to present my inquirer as someone who is seeking a good source of information, not just for whether p, but for this wider class? I would have to answer the question why he should (almost) always be doing that—the stronger the description of him the greater the problem of arguing that virtually any member of any community must satisfy it. But there may be a better route. For there seems to be at least a possibility that the concept constructed from my original basis will include the idea of the wider competence, or will be such as to imply this competence in nearly all cases. Then we will be able to say that the concept fashioned to meet the needs of my inquirer will put him in a position to declare a bonus: not only will he have found a good informant on the question whether p—he will usually have found an informant who is trustworthy over a range of p-like issues. Perhaps we shall end up saying that these two turn out the same, and that looking for a p-informant has to be equivalent to looking for a p-like inform-ant. But that is not clear a priori, and my first guess is that these two are not the same but only concomitant, and then only nearly always rather than invariably.

Let us investigate the guess. What the inquirer wants, we have seen, is someone possessing a (readily detectable) property which correlates well with being right as to whether p. More than that, the inquirer must believe that it correlates well, otherwise he can

[2] Ibid., p. 540.

make no use of the fact in selecting his informant. How is he to come by this belief?

One possibility is that he has found the potential informant to be right on this question in the past, and so believes that he will be right about it this time too. In this event it would be very unusual for his belief to be limited to just this one occasion; nearly always, if not actually always, he will believe that the potential informant is, and will be until some drastic change alters the situation, in general right as to whether p. But once he believes that, then he believes something about the informant's capacities beyond the present case, and immediately some concession has been made to the globalist view.

The concession isn't a very big one. So far as this argument goes, the class of propositions over which his expertise is taken to range might be very small indeed, though just how small depends on how we decide to count propositions. We shall have to consider a proposition whose truth-value may change, or at least one which the inquirer thinks may change. If we don't then our example can scarcely arise, for the inquirer, having once determined that the potential informant was right on that question, presumably knows the answer to it once and for all, or at least takes himself to do so, and will not appear again in the role of inquirer seeking an informant. But if we are talking about something which may change, then it could be said that what we have is in fact a changing series of questions expressible in the same terms, amounting as it were to 'whether p now (t_1)', 'whether p now (t_2)', and so on. We could adopt the alternative convention, and speak of one proposition's being assessed at different times, in which case it would sound as if our reliabilism was of the local rather than the global brand. Nothing really turns on this choice, of course; the solid point is that the inquirer's confidence in the informant will always in some measure extend beyond the single case which is his current concern.

The extension is too minimal, however, to give much support to McGinn's objection to Nozick.[3] Stronger support may be on the way, but before we look at it we may note that there are at any rate some cases in which there could be knowledge that p when the relevant class of 'p-like' truths doesn't reach beyond p itself, assessed at other times. Significantly, this occurs when the informant

[3] Ibid., p. 536.

stands in a unique relationship to the fact in question, or may be presumed to be uniquely familiar with it. An infant may know what its name is without knowing what anyone else's name is, and without knowing its age, and it may know its forename without knowing its surname. Being confident that someone knows their name doesn't help us to judge that they are valuable informants on many other questions, if any.

If we try hard enough we will probably be able to imagine circumstances in which we might reasonably trust a potential informant on the question whether there was a table in the next room, but not on the question whether there were chairs there, or anything else about the furniture. (In fact one doesn't even have to try very hard: suppose that he has never been in the room, but has just seen a table being carried through the door.) So if we are looking for strictly necessary conditions of being a good informant on any question whatever, we shall plump for localism and confine ourselves to the individual proposition at issue. But it is clear that all these examples are in some way exceptional, either in point of the proposition in question and the informant's particular relation to it, or of the circumstances in which he acquires the information. Far more common will be the case in which we trust him over p because we believe (or have found) him to be good at discerning the truth over a range of related matters. From up there in his tree Fred is good at telling where things are—indeed, people in general are good at it—it isn't any particular aptitude for spotting sabre-toothed tigers that we are relying on. If you are well placed to see enemies you are also well placed to see prey. In the vast majority of cases, if Fred is good for information on p, he will be good for information over a range of similar propositions. What counts for these purposes as similar to p will vary widely, but it is something which we are mostly pretty good at judging. If what makes me think that Fred is good for information on the colour of the mat is that I can see that he is looking at it, I will take him also to be good on the question whether the cat is on it or not; if he is in the next room and is a good informant about its colour because it is his house and his mat, I won't expect his reliability to extend to that question, but rather to others of a different type.

One could put it like this: on the basis of our estimate of the potential informant's capacities, situation and circumstances, we form an overall estimate of his belief-acquisition potential with respect to p. In nearly all cases the information we have used to estimate his potential with respect to p will justify an estimate of his potential with respect to quite a lot of other propositions as well. On different occasions (witness the above example) the factors that go into estimating his potential with respect to p may be different, although p is the same—they may be perceptual capacities on one occasion, inferential on another, a matter of his memory on a third, and in each case different considerations about his situation and circumstances will be pertinent. One effect is, of course, that the range of other propositions associated with reliability as to whether p will change accordingly; there will not be a static chunk of further information which invariably goes along with knowing whether p.

That thought necessitates an adjustment to what McGinn says about the pragmatic value of the concept of knowledge. It is not that once we know that Fred knows that p we can start using Fred's beliefs as to q and r as reliable indicators as well—the premise that he knows that p is too weak for this purpose. We have to know also the circumstances under which he came by his true belief as to whether p, since only this additional knowledge will allow us to judge which other propositions are so to speak 'adjacent' to p in this case. If you take me to know that there is a piano next door because I know the house, then other propositions about the furniture of that room are adjacent; if I know it because I heard the piano through a closed door, then those other propositions are not adjacent at all. It isn't, therefore, the concept of knowledge which has this pragmatic value; it is what one knows, on particular occasions, about how the knowledge was acquired.

This does something to explain a phenomenon that McGinn has latched onto:[4] the fact that one can generate counter-examples to Nozick's analysis by inventing cases in which the reliability (or 'track-

---

[4] Ibid. p. 536, with reference back to p. 533. A quotation may help the reader: 'Suppose you are surrounded by straight sticks immersed in water that therefore look bent to you; you, however, take them to be in air, and so you falsely believe of each of them that it is (really) bent. There is, though, one stick that is *not* immersed in water and it really *is* bent; on the basis of how that exceptional stick looks you believe it to be bent. Again, I take it that you do not *know* that that stick is bent, since, in view of the circumstances, your belief is only accidentally true. But Nozick's variation condition is satisfied in this case, since if *that* stick were not bent you would not believe it to be, because *it* would not, being in air and not water, look bent. So here we have a perceptual belief that tracks the truth of the believed proposition but does not rank as knowledge.'

ing') holds for p in particular but not for other propositions 'very like' p. Nozick's conditions are then satisfied, but we are unwilling to attribute knowledge of p. The example must be so constructed that the putative knower's capacities, and those features of his situation which might be thought to be making him reliable as to p, are such that one would be led to expect reliability with respect to these others as well. When it turns out that the subject is not reliable with respect to them, this makes us feel that it cannot really be those capacities etc. which are operative in respect of p, in spite of the fact that his belief 'tracks' its truth-value. We needn't therefore say that the reason why this is not knowledge is because knowledge of p calls for knowledge of the other ('p-like') propositions as well; we can say that even with respect to p the subject is not really exercising those capacities which make him reliable, so that we have to regard it as a fluke that he meets Nozick's conditions. And the trouble with flukes, from the point of view of the inquirer, is that they aren't predictable; which makes them of no use to him, since he needs to be able to tell in advance that there is a high chance of learning the truth.

This is paralleled by the line of thought that arises if we go back and look at McGinn's case from the perspective of our inquirer: if we now consider someone trying to use that person as an informant about whether p (whether a certain stick is bent or straight), we can see that they will judge him to be a good informant because they will see him looking at the objects in question, and since the properties he is judging them to have are (we suppose) simply perceptually detectable they take it that he possesses a property correlating well with being right as to whether p. What they learn, however, when they learn of his *incapacity* to give the right answer to the other questions (whether the other sticks are bent or straight) is that there is special reason to mistrust the correlation in this particular case. The question whether they—who don't at this stage, let us remember, know whether p or not—should regard him as a good informant is back in the melting pot. Unless they can find some further property which he possesses and which (i) correlates well with true belief as to p and (ii) doesn't correlate equally well with true belief as to all these other propositions about which—as we have now found out—he doesn't hold true beliefs, then they must suppose that his chances of telling them the truth about p are, for all they can tell, no better than random. And then, since their own

VIII

It has become common to distinguish between 'internalist' and 'externalist' accounts or analyses of knowledge. If we think of such an account as laying down necessary and sufficient conditions for knowing that p, first the truth of p, second the belief that p, third some further X which for these purposes we need not specify more closely, then an internalist will maintain that the knowing subject must have some kind of awareness of the fulfilment of the third condition, whereas an externalist takes it to be enough that the third condition hold, even if no thought of that condition, let alone belief about it, has ever crossed the subject's mind.

There is a widespread habit of thinking of some analyses as intrinsically internalist, others as intrinsically externalist. That, at any rate, is what I suspect, so I shall allow myself a paragraph to point out that it is not quite the case. The analysis in terms of justified true belief, or having evidence, or good reason, is internalist (so the story might go): having good reason to believe p involves having an awareness that some proposition q, also believed, bears a confirmatory relationship to p. On the other hand, the causal analysis (to take one example) only requires that the causal connection between the circumstance that p and the belief that p should in fact obtain. If the subject knows, or believes, that it obtains, well and good—but that is superfluous to the question of his knowledge that p. And the position is the same with the tracking analysis, reliabilism, and Unger's non-accidentalism.[1]

But in fact there is nothing intrinsic to any of these analyses which demands an internalist or an externalist treatment, and if they are attached to internalism and externalism in the way I have indicated that is more a matter of history than of their inner logic. Thus whether the classical 'true belief with a good reason' is internalist or not depends upon how one goes on to treat the notion of having good reason. Many philosophers, clearly, have taken it to involve

[1] P. Unger, (1).

awareness, on the part of the subject, both of the reason and of the fact that it is a good reason; but if one follows Dretske,[2] for instance, in analysing the possession of good reason in terms of the fulfilment of Nozick-like counterfactuals, then one finishes with the tracking analysis of knowing, and externalism at once becomes an obvious option. I say an option, rather than obligatory, because although the tracking analysis is standardly formulated externalistically, nothing about it prevents us, if we are so minded, from adding a clause to the effect that the subject must be aware that the counterfactuals hold; it is just that, recently, people haven't been so minded. Of course, there is one very serious problem for internalism: if it allows the awareness of the fulfilment of the third condition to become too strong, in other words to begin to look like a demand for *knowledge*, it is threatened with regress. But that is not a problem that arises for some particular analyses and not for others; we meet it once we try to take any analysis in an internalist version. And this we can do: it is worth remembering that Goldman's original statement of the causal theory spoke of the need for the subject to be able to 'reconstruct' the causal chain in its important links—which introduces an internalist element, at least on the obvious interpretation of what such reconstruction would amount to.

At first sight it looks as if our approach is bound to favour externalist theories: will not the characterisation of the good informant be externalist? After all, if we judge Fred to have a property that correlates well with having the truth as to whether p, we shall judge him to be a good informant quite independently of whether he is himself aware of having that property or of its correlation with the truth of his belief.

Before accepting that, there is one possible counter to it that we should dispose of. Earlier, in Section II, we wondered whether a good informant might not need to be someone who offers his opinion confidently. Should the question be raised anew at this point in the argument? Might not that confidence call for awareness that one possesses a property correlating closely with being right on the matter in hand? If so, would that not put internalism in an analysis much on a par with what was then under discussion: the inclusion of the belief condition?

If we are really thinking of an internalist *analysis*, in which the

---

[2] F. Dretske.

subject's awareness is to be laid down as a logically necessary condition, the answer would surely be negative. Confident belief can certainly exist in the absence of awareness of those properties of oneself which justify the confidence, or make it very likely that the belief is true. Things may not be quite so clear cut if we take the question strictly as put, that is as asking whether internalism may not have the same kind of status as the belief condition; for doubtless in the vast majority of cases people are aware of some such property, and this (contingent) fact about confident informants must have an effect on the way in which we think of them. (This, according to the argument of Section IV, is what underlies the plausibility of the traditional analysis in terms of justification or reasons.) But be that as it may, we have still found one point on which the supporter of the belief-condition can call which has no analogue for the internalist: the lack of belief seriously disrupts our willingness to think of the subject as an informant rather than an evidential source of information. In part, at least, this happens because we are then reluctant to regard him as properly *telling* us whatever it is that he says. The failure of the internalist condition, on the other hand, has no tendency in that direction.

So the view that our approach will at least in some degree favour externalism is right, I think. But perhaps it is only right so long as we stay with the third-person perspective, and concentrate on the case in which someone is trying to decide of someone else whether or not they are a trustworthy informant. In some respects at least the position changes if we look at the situation that obtains when someone has to make this decision about themselves.

At the beginning of this essay I argued that consideration of the third-person case was the sounder starting point. If one finds oneself with a belief as to whether p, I said, that pre-empts inquiry; no search for an informant will begin. But I also hinted that slightly more sophisticated states of mind might bring the first-person question into focus; and it can easily be seen how, in the primitive situation that we first imagined, such states of mind could arise. For one thing, there will be circumstances in which a group is looking for an informant on some issue: who knows whether p? And it will be important to have a practice whereby people sometimes declare themselves to be qualified, since it will often arise that they are themselves the only person in a position to tell whether they are qualified or not. That would be so, for instance, if the question relates to what happened at a certain place at a certain time; it may well be that the only person aware that Fred was there then is Fred himself. Or again, it may well be that nobody but Fred is aware that he has just seen a signpost.

Now an immediate reaction might be that all Fred needs to do is to offer an opinion as to whether p, either to assert that p, or to assert that not-p, and that this doesn't involve turning the concept of knowledge, or of being a good informant for the group to follow, on himself. Sometimes, perhaps, but there will be many cases in which the bald assertion only provokes further challenges—how do you know, what makes you think that, Fred?—and the fact that this is likely will induce people to consider their defence in advance, which means considering whether or not they themselves are informants acceptable to the group. Then it is perfectly understandable that they should often announce themselves as such in the first place. Who knows whether p? And Fred replies: I do. And there is another reason why the practice of asserting (or denying) p cannot always do the job: the group may wish its attention drawn to a sound informant on some general topic, before any particular question has been decided upon.

In addition to that, we are not infallible. Some of our beliefs are false, and what is more, we pretty soon make that discovery for ourselves, even if others don't force it upon us first, which they very well may. So we shall develop a practically based interest in whether we ourselves are good informants; as in the third-person case, the interest will be sharper where the practical importance of having a true belief is greater. We shall sometimes be interested, therefore, in asking of beliefs that we have, whether they are to be relied upon; and, perhaps more often, in cases in which we want a belief as to whether p but don't have one, we shall be keen to acquire one in a way which makes it likely to be true when we get it. And in this latter case it may be much more convenient to set about making ourselves good informants directly than to try to find someone else who is one. One great advantage of using yourself as an informant, of course, is that unlike everybody else you are always around; and in any case you are sure to be the first person you ask.

There is therefore nothing about the method of practical explication which disallows consideration of the first-person case; on the contrary, it can be seen to be a legitimate, indeed a required, extension of the approach. But once we do consider it we can see immediately how the tendency to internalism arises. Internalism consists in adding to the third condition (or so interpreting it that it implies) a clause to the effect that the subject is aware of possessing X—having good reason for his belief, or whatever. The self-directed, or first-personal, inquiry brings us into the neighbourhood of internalism because it forces on us the question 'Do I meet the third condition?'; and to decide that we do, or that we are good informants, we must satisfy ourselves that the answer is 'Yes'. Then we are in just that extra state which internalism characteristically adds to the externalist account.

I say 'brings us into the neighbourhood of' rather than 'brings us to' internalism because the fact that we are in that extra state doesn't oblige us to build it into the concept. But the self-directed nature of the investigation—it is ourselves we are aiming at certifying—brings the extra state on to the scene in a particularly seductive way: I cannot get into a position to certify myself a good informant with respect to p unless I consider whether I meet the condition X and decide positively. And this is easily confused with the thought that being a good informant involves being aware, or at the very least believing, that one fulfils the third condition. In the third-person investigation the opportunity for the confusion does not arise. If I am to certify Fred a good informant then I must satisfy myself that Fred fulfils (3); but to confuse that with the claim that Fred must satisfy himself of that as well is (happily) too gross to be troublesome.

In case any reader is unconvinced that the former confusion is tempting, I shall say a few words about a parallel confusion which can easily be documented. Not only is it parallel, it is closely related—indeed it may at bottom even be identical. I refer to the much discussed question of epistemic logic, whether or not knowing that p entails knowing that one knows that p. I shall call it the 'Iteration Principle': Kp entails KKp. It is not difficult to see that this question is very closely related to the one we have just started from, namely whether to give an internalist or externalist analysis of knowledge. If we think schematically of an analysis of knowledge as consisting of the truth condition, the belief condition, and some further (perhaps complex) condition which we refer to as '(3)', then Internalism is characterised by the thesis that to know that p the subject must know that (3). The Iteration Principle holds that too, but adds that there must be knowledge of the two preceding conditions as well.

That an externalist will return an immediate 'No' to Iteration is clear enough; just a little more thought is needed to appreciate the force of the temptation for the internalist to answer 'Yes'. If to know that p is to satisfy the conditions:

(1) p
(2) S believes that p
(3) S has X

then knowing that one knows is to know that the three conditions hold, that is to say:

(1′) S knows that p
(2′) S knows that S believes that p
(3′) S knows that S has X

Now if an internalist so understands (3) that he does not really distinguish it from (3′), then little else is needed to effect the passage from knowing, {1 & 2 & 3}, to knowing that one knows: {1′ & 2′ & 3′}. Since (3) is true, our internalist will take it that (3′) is true. Since *ex hypothesi* the conjunction {1 & 2 & 3} holds, and he takes that conjunction to define knowing, he will take it that (1′) holds. Now only (2′) remains to be accounted for. Our internalist might take that step as a result of believing something like the traditional thesis of the transparency of our mental states to consciousness—that we always know what we believe. But without accepting that dubious thesis, he might get to (2′) as a common-sense consequence of believing (3′). For if his chosen X is 'has good reason to believe that p', and S knows that he has it—which is what (3′) says—then S is hardly likely to miss the fact—(2)—that he believes that p. So (2′) will hold, and with it the full set of conditions for knowing that one knows. If the chosen X, as in the causal theory or the tracking analysis, actually mentions the belief that p, the passage to (2′) is even more obvious. So it should not be in the slightest bit surprising if the internalist takes the view that 'S knows that p' and 'S knows that S knows that p' are equivalent (though he might, because of the status of (2′), resist the conclusion that the equivalence is strictly speaking a two-way entailment).

Now at least with regard to the 'If Kp then KKp' principle we can certainly find examples of just the confusion under discussion.

Here are two from Hintikka's *Knowledge and Belief*, one quoted (approvingly) by him, the other actually used.[3] Schopenhauer, in *On the Fourfold Root...*, writes:

... just try... to know without knowing that you know .. ,[4]

—a challenge the force of which must surely rely on the hope that your attempts to know will include attempts to assure yourself that you know, and the further hope that this will convince you that knowing itself includes knowing that you know. The joker here, of course, is the second word. If we *try* to know that *p* we are going to concentrate our minds on the question whether we know that *p* and what we have to do to bring that state of affairs about. Then, if our efforts go well, we very likely shall finish up knowing that we know that *p*. At least it will be the case that we know that *p*, we shall believe that we know that *p*, and we shall be in a state such that people in that state who believe that they know that *p* virtually always believe truly.

But it is not the knowing that has produced the iteration; it is the trying. Think of someone who, instead of trying to know that *p*, tries to find out simply whether *p*. If he does the job well, he will end up knowing that *p* (or not-*p* as the case may be). At any rate, he will arrive at a true belief and a state which correlates well with truth in beliefs of that type. But whether he will know that he knows is quite another matter, depending on how self-conscious his investigation of *p* was; he may, but quite likely he won't. Hintikka himself uses a similar route:

... all those circumstances which would justify one in saying 'I know' will also justify one in saying 'I know that I know'.[5]

Now the joker is justification. Does it smuggle in internalism? Am I justified in saying 'I know that *p*' just because I do know that *p*? Or, as is plausible, is something else needed? For if it is, it may be the something else, and not just the fact of my knowledge that *p*, that entails the knowledge of the knowledge—assuming, that is, that anything about the situation has this consequence, which is far from clear. What is, I think, clear, is that if I set out to be justified in saying 'I know that *p*' I will almost certainly aim at

[3] J. Hintikka. See pp. 108, 111.
[4] A. Schopenhauer, ch. VII, Sect. 41, cited in J. Hintikka, p. 108.
[5] J. Hintikka, p. 111.

getting into a position in which even the internalist would agree
that I satisfy the conditions for knowledge; and if successful I shall
end up knowing that I know. But that has nothing to do either
with the question whether internalism is correct or with the Iteration
Principle. It is after all true for any value of p, not just for ones
that contain an occurrence of 'knows that', that if I set out to be
justified in saying that p I shall (assuming competence) very likely
finish up knowing that p (unless, question-beggingly, internalism
be assumed); but it does not follow that p can only be true if I
know that p. Omniscience does not come that easily.

We have seen that there will often be motives, arising in the primitive situation or state of nature, to apply the concept of the informant
to oneself. This does not mean that there is anything fundamentally
first-personal or fundamentally third-personal about the concept of
knowledge. The informant whose credentials are under scrutiny may
be either oneself or another. But this very impartiality between first
and third person perspectives does, I think, speak in support of
those who offer externalist accounts of the concept. The third-person
view certainly favours externalism, whereas the hint of internalism
experienced in the first-person case gives no sufficient reason to
break the semantic symmetry and posit a different, because internalist, concept that one applies to oneself. For the hint of internalism
can be accounted for without supposing that one is then asking,
of oneself, a question with an internalist content. Simplicity and
elegance favour reading the question—am I a good informant with
respect to p?—externalistically, and seeing the internalist aura as
an unsurprising consequence of the fact that it is here being asked
internally, that is to say, of oneself.

The concept of the good informant, I have argued, has the property that once we try to state specific necessary and sufficient conditions for it, once we add some specific condition Y to the requirement that the informant believe the truth on the matter at issue, it proves possible to 'outflank' the attempted analysis: we can imagine further facts, compatible with the informant's possessing Y, such that when they are included in the picture his rating drops to an unacceptable level; so the suggested conditions—true belief plus Y—were not, after all, sufficient.

We noted that the recent literature on the analysis of the concept of knowledge suggests something suspiciously similar: when a specific analysis is proposed, sooner or later someone devises a counter-example to demonstrate the insufficiency of the proposed conditions. A very general and approximate description of these counter-examples might be: they all present possible circumstances in which the further condition X is satisfied, but satisfied in such a way that it becomes accidental that the subject holds a true belief as to whether p. What, with more precision, does this really amount to?

Gettier addressed himself to the 'justified true belief' (JTB) analysis. A condition of the construction of his type of counter-example, he pointed out, was that it should be logically possible to have a justified belief in a proposition that is in fact false—S is justified in believing that p is not to entail that p is true. This being granted (it is not easy to resist it without having to admit that justification is an unnecessarily strong requirement) Gettier proceeds to invent situations in which the subject is indeed justified, but in which, given the manner in which the justification arises, the likelihood that he is right as to whether p is not thereby increased.

This makes the JTB analysis—granted Gettier's principle about justification—structurally very similar to the conditions on a good informant: true belief plus possession of some property which lends high probability to truth of belief, but does not (because such a requirement would be too strong to be a necessary condition) entail truth of belief.

It seems plausible to say that a third condition which did not lend high probability to truth of the belief could not (taken with the earlier conditions) be sufficient for knowledge. It looks, in other words, as if a crucial part of the role of the third condition (whatever else it may need to do, if anything) is to provide this probability. That being granted, it can be seen that such an analysis will always be vulnerable to counter-examples that work by adding further circumstances compatible with the third condition and which, when added, leave that probability unacceptably low. To this we must add the caveat, however: provided the third condition in question does not entail that the subject's belief is true—for then no such further circumstances will be conceivable.

The caveat suggests two continuations. Not only the JTB analysis, but the other three principal contenders as well seem to be indefinitely open to 'non-sufficiency proofs' by counter-example; so we shall have to ask whether they share with it the relevant property—that their proposed third conditions do not entail the truth of the subject's belief. And as a preliminary it might be as well to ask whether the JTB analysis may not have an acceptable version which lacks that property, that is, one which uses a notion of justification according to which justification entails truth.

The first thought, already mentioned, is that any such concept of justification would be far too strong to be necessary. Using it in the analysis would amount to the demand that the subject be in possession of evidence which entails the truth of p. But that demand is met in so few cases that the analysis would decisively rule out virtually everything, and such a misfit between what actually is knowledge and what is normally taken to be knowledge is drastic enough to kill the proposed analysis.

For the time being, I think, we have to agree with that. Admittedly, until we have decided what features of use and usage are constitutive of a concept it would be premature to decree it unthinkable that nearly every application of some concept should be wrong. But someone who wishes to analyse knowledge in such a way that, if he were right, that would actually be the case, surely owes us some half-way plausible hypothesis about how the massive misfit could have come about. If it were 'witch' that we were talking about, then the debt could be settled: there is a very natural—though somewhat pathological—explanation of the fact that the word acquired such a meaning as not to apply to any of the many persons to whom it was applied, and was applied to them nevertheless. But the concept of knowledge doesn't look anything like so tractable, and until there is a story about it having something approaching the plausibility of the obvious one about 'witch' we should provisionally assume the worst.

It might be suggested, however, that the concept of justification be handled rather differently. Could we not say that a lower standard of evidence than deductive entailment of the conclusion is sufficient, but that it is also a necessary condition of justification that the belief actually be true? So even very good evidence for p would not properly be called justification of the belief that p if that belief turned out to be false. If this were the concept of justification used as the third condition of the JTB analysis then the third condition would entail truth of belief, but knowledge would not call for evidence so good as to entail the proposition known.

There is no escape down this route. It makes the concept of justification as it were bipartite: (i) S has good evidence for p, (ii) p is true. So the JTB analysis, using this conception of justification, renders 'S knows that p' as:

(1) p is true
(2) S believes that p
(3) (i) S has good evidence for p
    (ii) p is true

Since (3)(ii) duplicates (1) its effect is merely nominal. The same counter-examples as Gettier used against the sufficiency of JTB as he wished it understood can be used again, with exactly the same result. But there is another modification to the JTB analysis, widely known as the 'no false lemma' principle, which is far from nominal. Since the salvage which it promises—if it works at all—extends to other types of analysis than JTB, I postpone consideration of it until the end of the section. For the moment we may move on to look at the recent alternative analyses, the causal theory, the tracking theory and reliabilism.

To the true belief that p the causal theory adds a causal connection between the belief and the fact that p. It may—in fact must—go on to place restricting conditions on the sort of causal connection allowed (it must not be 'deviant'), or on the subject's position in regard to it (Goldman: he must be able to 'reconstruct' its essential links correctly). But whatever these restrictions are they do not affect the point that the existence of any causal connection with the fact that p entails that p is a fact, hence that the subject's belief that p is true. So the third condition does not merely make the truth of the belief probable; it entails it. The structural parallel with the JTB analysis is lost, and with it our neat explanation of why the causal analysis too seems to be indefinitely counter-exemplifiable.

The same is true of the Nozick–Dretske analysis, which adds the two counterfactual conditionals to the requirement of true belief. They entail that the subject's belief that p is true, not merely that its truth is highly probable. Yet again we find it possible to invent odd (or 'deviant') ways of satisfying them which indicate that they do not combine with true belief to give logically sufficient conditions for knowledge.

Reliabilism adds to true belief the need for the belief to have been formed 'by a reliable method'. Here various well-known questions arise. First, it is not clear how we determine the method by which a given belief was formed, for there will have been a highly complex process which can correctly be described in many ways. Under some descriptions it will be reliable—acquisition of the belief that p by *that* kind of process will (nearly) always lead to truth—under others, equally correct descriptions of it, it will not be. The easy way out, to say that a belief was acquired by a reliable method if there is *some* true description of the process under which it is reliable, is not as easy as it looks, for there will always be some description of that kind unless we make further provisions setting limits on what is to count for these purposes as a description of the process. Thus 'guessing' might be a description of the process, but 'guessing correctly' had better not be, even when the subject did guess correctly. (Even the way in which Bernard Williams's company chairman[1] came to believe that the accountant was depressed was, if described in sufficient and properly chosen detail, a way of coming to that belief which would always lead to truth.)

Suppose we have solved this problem, so that we know which descriptions of a process of belief-acquisition count as specifying 'the method(s)' by which the belief was acquired. Then the process

---

[1] See Section VI.

will be as reliable as its most reliable specification, that is the one (or 'ones' if there is a tie) under which it has the best chance of issuing in a true belief. The next question is: how good does that chance have to be for the process to be 'reliable'? Must every process satisfying that description lead to a true belief, and if so are we speaking of every actual, or of every possible process? Must it (either way) be every process, or will it do if it leads to a true belief in the vast majority of cases? Are we only speaking of the cases in which it is applied to settling the precise question whether p, or are we also thinking of investigations of other propositions of the same type as p? If the latter, how do we decide which propositions are 'of the same type' as p?

Fortunately we don't, for the moment at least, have to decide all or any of these questions on the reliabilist's behalf. Unless he calls for a method so reliable that it would lead to a true belief about p on any possible occasion on which it might be applied to that question then it will always be possible to think of further circumstances such that, even though the subject had reached his belief about p by a reliable method, his chances of being right about p were not (given these further circumstances) thereby improved. And this will leave reliabilism open to counter-examples showing it not to offer sufficient conditions for knowing.

Are there any prospects for the reliabilist in taking the stronger line and calling for a method that would yield the truth about p under all circumstances, possible as well as actual? In theory it would be open to him to try something analogous to our JTB-theorist who wanted to make justification a matter of two logically independent components, one being possession of adequate evidence and the other the *de facto* truth of the belief. What this comes to is that identification of the method would include the fact that it had succeeded; so that any attempt which ended in a false belief, however similar to the first in other respects, would be said not to involve the use of the same method.

Quite apart from the weirdness of such a use of 'same method', this clumsy manœuvre achieves nothing, for the reason that we saw in the parallel treatment of 'justification'. The reliabilist has now defined knowledge like this:

(1) p is true
(2) S believes that p

(3) (i) S acquired the belief that p by doing X
     (ii) S's belief that p is true

where doing X is something that correlates well with, but does not entail, forming a true belief as to whether p. And once again (3)(ii) is redundant, since it just recapitulates the conjunction of (1) and (2). The same counter-examples as would demonstrate the insufficiency of {(1) & (2) & (3)(i)} do the same after the addition of (3)(ii)—for (3)(ii) adds nothing.

There are, however, some descriptions of processes leading to belief that entail the truth of the belief without falling apart into two components, one not entailing the truth of the belief and the other just explicitly stating that the belief is true. Many beliefs, we all suppose, have as an essential part of their cause the state of affairs which is their object. As we have seen, this description of the process of belief-acquisition does entail the truth of the belief acquired; and it does not decompose into two independent conditions, such as:

(3) (i) S's belief that p was caused
     (ii) p is a fact

So it seems that a reliabilist might say that a 'reliable method' was indeed one that couldn't fail, and allow as productive of knowledge only such processes as are susceptible of that kind of description. He would admit causal processes involving connection with the fact believed, processes that 'would lead to the belief that p if and only if p', processes involving the due consideration of reasons logically sufficient for p, and perhaps not much else, unless he could think of some new and plausible analysis. What he is doing, clearly, is borrowing (in one case in strengthened form) the analyses already in circulation and disjoining them. To summarise these possibilities:

(1) Reliabilism calls on processes which have (only) a very good chance of delivering true belief.
(2) Reliabilism disjoins the existing analyses, in one case (JTB) taking a strengthened form of the third condition—and thus achieves a logical guarantee of truth.
(3) Reliabilism suggests that there are other descriptions of processes leading to belief such that any process satisfying them must (logically) deliver truth.

In the case of (1), as soon as anything specific is suggested there will appear 'Gettier-like' counter-examples, for the reasons given. In the case of (2) there is nothing new to look at. In the case of (3) we must wait to see what these descriptions are, bearing in mind the while that (*a*) there will be no point to them if they are of the sort that build in the truth of the belief as an independent condition, and (*b*) that the reliabilist must not overstretch what counts as the description of a process—on pain of having all true belief turn into knowledge.

That out of the way, at least until further notice, we can return to the causal analysis. Here the third condition (C) does entail (not just give high probability) that S's belief that p is true. So when the conditions turn out insufficient that cannot be explained just as the concept of the good informant suggests, by saying that in the counter-examples we are adding further compatible information (FCI) such that {(FCI) & (C)} does not lend high probability to 'S is right that p'. Since in this case (C) entails 'S is right that p', so does the conjunction of (C) with any (FCI).

Nevertheless, I believe that the original intuition is correct: what bothers us about the 'deviant causal chains' examples is that they present cases in which the attainment of a true belief that p, even by a process causally connected with the fact that p, is a fluke or accident. In some sense, it was very unlikely to turn out that way. We may look at another counter-example proposed by Bernard Williams in the paper already cited. Admittedly, Williams characterised it precisely as a case in which the truth of the belief was not an accident, but this shouldn't put us off; it just shows that the concept of being an accident is a slippery one—I shall argue for a different application of it. First the example:

A, being from Guinea, tells B falsely that he is from Ghana; but (let us fancifully suppose) owing to features of A's spoken English which are peculiar to Guineans, B takes him to have said 'Guinea' when he said 'Ghana'.

Now B has come to believe (what is true) that A is from Guinea, and (so Williams continues) 'it is no accident, relative to A's being from Guinea, that this has come about'. What we can certainly agree is that the fact of A's being from Guinea plays a causal role in the process leading to B's belief—that was how A came by the peculiarity of accent. But can we not also agree, looking at the process, that there was something deeply accidental, or coincidental, or unlikely, about B's having arrived at a true belief rather than a false one?

First, A had to choose the spoken word for conveying his information; secondly, when he shaped up to tell his lie he had to hit on precisely that country the English name of which would sound to B like 'Guinea' when pronounced with a Guinean accent. Nigeria wouldn't have done, nor would Ethiopia or Zimbabwe or (probably) anything else, but—it just happened to be 'Ghana' that he picked on. Well, well! Relative to the evidence in our possession—and that is what judgements of probability are relative to—B was extremely unlikely to acquire a true belief. But the unlikely can happen; and this time it did.

Make the comparison: let there be a chair here, and suppose that I look at it attentively. Now, what has to happen for me to *fail* to acquire the belief that there is a chair here? Answer: something pretty unusual. Let there be a Guinean here intent on deceiving me about his origins, and suppose that I listen to what he tells me and believe what I understand him to say. What has to happen for me to acquire the right belief (without benefit of knowing that he is lying, without benefit of experience of the Guinean accent)? Answer: something pretty extraordinary. Wasn't he unlucky? Of course he was—the odds were piled house-high in his favour.

We find much the same if we look again at one of Williams' other examples, that of the Chairman of the Board. People who are depressed characteristically have a certain type of facial expression, a certain heaviness of bodily movement, a certain style of speech, an absence of energy and initiative, a certain 'slant' on life and its questions. Someone who detects these features in the normal way and infers, if he finds them, that their possessor is depressed, has a reasonably good chance of forming a true belief. But our chairman didn't do this; he came by his (true) belief only because the accountant, of all the ways in which he might have manifested his depression, happened to come up with one (of the very few, we may presume), which had the effect of making him (the chairman) depressed. And he had to come up with it for the reason that he (the accountant) was depressed, rather than for the reason which must be at least equally common: that (in his everyday professional state of mind) he had seen that the firm's state was actually parlous. The chairman's chances of ending up with a true belief would have to be assessed as very slender by anyone who did not already know the whole story, including the facts about the accountant's state of mind.

What seemed to cause a problem here was the wrong approach

to chance. Of course, given the premise that I acquired the belief that p by causal connection with the fact that p we can conclude deductively that I acquired a true belief. But whether it was only to be expected that I would acquire a true belief, or whether on the contrary I needed the luck of the devil himself, is a question not touched by that premise or the deduction we can trivially make from it. What the counter-examples do is move the believer to the lucky end of the scale; they present situations in which he gets things right against all the odds. 'Deviant' causes produce counter-examples to the sufficiency of the analysis precisely for that reason, and their permanent availability is due to the very feature of probability judgements which, as we have seen, has just the same effect on any attempt to specify conditions logically sufficient for qualifying as a good informant.

It is now time to redeem a promise given earlier in the section. In Gettier's original counter-examples to the sufficiency of the JTB analysis, a subject reasons admirably but reaches a conclusion which is in fact false. From this falsehood he then draws (with unexceptionable logic) a further inference which happens to yield a truth. The ensuing discussion of such cases therefore lead very naturally to modification of the analysis by addition of the 'No false lemma' (NFL) principle associated in particular with the names of Keith Lehrer and Gilbert Harman.[2] Not only must the subject have good reasons for his belief; the train of reasoning which leads him to it must not include anything which is, in fact, false. Thus we cut out Gettier-cases at what looks very like the root.

It soon becomes clear that the principle itself had better be modified a little. As stated above it can only be applied to cases in which we are able to identify the particular train of thought through which the subject passed in getting to the belief. So a reformulation in conditional terms comes to be preferred: there must be no proposition, which is in fact false, such that if the subject came to learn that it was false he would no longer take himself to have good reason to believe that p and would accordingly drop the belief. And if this be found objectionable on the grounds that it idealises the rationality of the subject—who is required first to see that the new evidence leaves him without good reason for p, and then having seen that

---

[2] See G. Harman, pp. 47–9 and *passim*, and K. Lehrer. It is interesting to compare F. P. Ramsey.

to stop believing p—we can reformulate again in more objective terms: if he learnt that the said falsehood was false he would no longer be justified in believing that p. (With this we are very close to the version favoured by Lehrer.)[3]

Now it is clear enough how the Gettier examples trade upon the existence of the false belief to make it only accidental—in spite of his excellent reasons—that the subject ends up with a truth. Good reasons, as I have said, will at best only preserve truth; once it is lost they have no power of their own to regenerate it out of falsehood, and only the lucky concurrence of circumstances can do it for them. So one can see the role of falsehood here, and the sense behind ruling it out if one wants to arrive at logically sufficient conditions for knowledge. That makes it sound as if the 'No false lemma' principle must be a necessary condition for knowledge; but the matter is not so simple—we shall return to it. For the moment we may concentrate on the question whether it is sufficient, or more precisely: If we add it as reinforcement to justified true belief, do we then reach a set of conditions that are logically sufficient for 'S knows that p'? Is there any other way in which the subject's belief that p, whilst true, could be true only accidentally?

I think that the following, at least, can be said: if we know of a potential informant both that his belief as to whether p is based on good reasons and that he satisfies the NFL condition, then we may deduce that it is very probable that he is right in his belief. If all we knew were just that he has good reasons for believing that p (or that not-p), then we could not deduce any such thing, because there might be some further truth such that if it were added to our evidence we would no longer regard his being right as very likely at all. It should be clear, however, that this (the addition of something else to our evidence) is the only way in which our estimate of the probability can be lowered, given the idealisation that we are operating rationally. (There is nothing remarkable about this exhaustiveness—if we are operating rationally we will not change the estimate unless there is a change in the evidence.) But coming to believe a further truth is *ipso facto* coming to realise that some falsehood is false—the falsehood, namely, which the negation of that very truth expresses. So if we say, by imposing the No-false-lemma requirement, that there is no such falsehood, then we in

³ K. Lehrer, p. 174.

effect say that there is no truth competent to disturb the original estimate of probability based on the fact that the subject has good reasons, which must therefore remain high.

It appears, then, that the NFL condition is immensely powerful. It would be very surprising if its addition to the analysis of knowledge as justified true belief—or to any other—did not result in sufficient conditions for knowledge. For if we take any condition X such that on the evidence that S has X we would regard it as highly probable that S's belief as to whether p is true, and then add to X that there is no false lemma, this guarantees that the probability will remain high whatever new facts come to light. And that, given our core hypothesis, ought to be sufficient for the situation to strike us as an intuitively satisfactory case of knowledge.

Of course, the very power of the NFL condition exposes it to a threat from the other direction. So broad is its blanket that no inquirer will ever have it in his grasp. Along with recognising the property X of the potential informant on which he rightly makes his original high estimate of the chances of getting to hear the truth, he also has to know that there is no further truth such that, going on the conjunction of it with X, he would (again rightly) significantly reduce the estimated value. That calls for a kind of near-omniscience on the inquirer's part, and the call has two obvious disadvantages. First, we can be quite sure that it will never in practice be answered: no inquirer ever has that much knowledge. Secondly, if some imaginary inquirer did have it, and if it played an essential part in his decision to accept that person as likely to offer the truth as to p, his approach to the 'informant' would look much more like the approach to a source of information.[4]

And if the NFL condition is so powerful, what of our earlier impression that it is a necessary condition for knowledge? That impression was based on the argument that, if the subject acquires a true belief as the conclusion of a chain of reasoning which at some point involves a false premise, then the truth of his belief is accidental: reasoning has power to preserve the likelihood of truth, but not to restore it.

Now this argument does seem to me to hold if we are thinking of the categorical version of the NFL principle, that is to say the version according to which the subject must not have engaged in

[4] See Section V.

any actual process of reasoning that made essential use of a falsehood. But we have observed that its proponents are, understandably, not very keen on this version of the principle, for reasons indicated at the beginning of this section. More substantively, adding the NFL principle in this form to the standard JTB analysis does not yield sufficient conditions. One reason for that is that it may be satisfied trivially in those cases in which the belief arises without mediation of any process of reasoning, as in perception—where nevertheless Gettier-like examples can still be composed. But another is that we may imagine our subject to reach the belief that p by reasoning that makes perfectly acceptable use of a very restricted range of premises, negligently giving not a thought to a number of other facts with which he is very familiar. Had he taken them into account he would never have come to believe that p, since taken in its entirety his evidence speaks strongly against it. But, freakishly, his total corpus of relevant evidence is misleading—p is in fact true, for reasons of which he knows nothing. Not many will want to say that he knows that p; but he certainly satisfies the categorical version of the No-false-lemma condition.

We turn therefore to the counterfactual formulation of the principle. It may give us sufficient conditions—as I have argued, we should certainly expect it to do so—but is it, so to speak, really necessary? I very much doubt it. I would expect there to be plenty of cases in which we would feel at least strongly inclined to ascribe knowledge when it is not satisfied. The basic recipe is as follows:

Begin by letting S have very strong evidence (call it all E) for p, and let him believe that p on the basis of this evidence. We may imagine it to be as strong as we like, provided it does not actually entail the truth of p. Now let there be some other truth, D, such that on the basis of (E & D) S would rate p much less likely. D has always been a very good guide to the truth of not-p (though again, not a deductively valid one), and had S come to believe it (in addition to all of E) he would have fallen into complete confusion as to what to think about p. But on this occasion the discovery of D would have been merely misleading: in the unique circumstances now obtaining it lacks its usual connections with not-p.

Examples cooked to this recipe fail the counterfactual form of the NFL principle: not-D is the false lemma in question. But in many such examples it will feel perfectly natural to say that the subject knows that p, even though he would not have known it (or even believed it) had he had the sheer bad luck to have the totally misleading matter of D brought to his attention—and brought to his attention by itself, so that he was not in a position to judge that D was, just this once, nothing but a red herring.

In summary: the No false lemma principle may be taken in a form in which it is indeed necessary, but then adding it does not yield sufficient conditions. Or it may be taken in a form in which it combines with JTB (and, I suggest, with pretty well anything else ever seriously advanced) to give a set of sufficient conditions; but in that form it is not necessary. The conjecture derived from our 'practical explication', that one will achieve sufficiency only by including conditions too strong to be necessary, survives this test.

X

Certain cases noticed earlier threaten trouble for our hypothesis.[1] There was Luigi, who knows exactly what happened to Mario, but is no use as an informant—he's not telling. There was Matilda, who knows (this time) that the house is on fire, but is no use any more as an informant because nobody believes a word she says. There is the secretly studious milkman, who actually knows the answer to the abstruse question that is bothering you, but is no good as an informant because nothing about him gives the slightest hint that it would be anything but stupid to ask him. (Even his best friends were never aware that he once swotted the topic up when a reserve for a heat of Mastermind.) Remember also Colin Radford's French Canadian: who would have guessed, before they chanced to start on that game, that there was the slightest point in asking him even the simplest question about British history?

In all these cases a gap seems to open up between our natural ascriptions of knowledge and the concept we have arrived at by considering the practical situation of the inquirer seeking an informant. To come to grips with them, we need to step back from the concept of knowledge, and from that of a good informant as well, in order to look at a far more general principle very widely involved in concept-formation. It is what I shall call the principle of objectivisation, and it will prove fecund enough not only to help us understand the types of case just mentioned but also to offer insight into a phenomenon at first sight quite unrelated to them: the existence and durability of philosophical scepticism.

We start off in terms as general as possible. A creature has a certain need and desires its satisfaction. What it wants is something which, there and then, will satisfy the need; and unless it is the sort of thing which just comes completely unbidden, the creature must be able to register it as such so as to be able to orientate its behaviour

---

[1] See Section II, last para.

towards it, and it must have the necessary motor-capacities to do so. It needs this situation as a whole—if it all obtains, the creature succeeds, if any of it is missing, the creature fails and the need persists. So if all we are thinking of is the fulfilment of this need here and now, it has no cause to distinguish the various aspects: the presence of food, its own capacity to be nourished by that food, its own capacity to detect the food and reach it. Thus, perhaps, the barnacle. But with the slightest hint of intelligence this primitive holism starts to fragment. The creature must distinguish between food, here, now, provided it makes the right movement, and food here, soon, provided it waits very quietly for a bit and then makes the right movement. It must distinguish these from food, there, soon, provided it can get there; and cases in which it can get there from ones in which it cannot. Helpful again, as life grows more varied, will be the capacity to distinguish cases in which it simply cannot get there from those in which it cannot get there because of some temporary hindrance, either in the environment or in itself. These are differences in the situation which require different strategies, and the creature which can respond to each of them appropriately will be more likely to prosper.

That creature was an individualist. If we place it in a social group the possibilities expand again. What it cannot reach perhaps a maturer individual can—which suggests an all too familiar way of getting at food that would otherwise be inaccessible: point it out to Mum. Others may be better than it at recognising food; so far as they seem trustworthy, follow their recommendations. Others may be able to use substances as food which it cannot; see that they get it. (That will be encouraged by the existence of natural altruism, if there be any, but it can and will arise without it: it isn't necessarily for the sake of the horse that we give it the oats instead of eating them ourselves.)

What we see here are the natural pressures driving thought away from the totally subjectivist stance, the pure 'here and now for me as I am here and now' that I slanderously imputed to the barnacle. They induce the thought of the satisfaction of a need at other times and other places—whether that be the present need or a similar need expected for the future, the thought of recognitional and behavioural (and maybe digestive) capacities other than those I have here and now, and hence of an object which can in the right circumstances satisfy such needs whilst, for any number of reasons, coming nowhere near to meeting the wholly subjectivised conditions from which our thought-experiment began.

One more everyday example, before we turn to informants. I may well be interested in 'something which I can now sit on' (only close and accessible objects need apply). But in due course I shall be interested, since I anticipate wanting to sit down at future times, in objects which I could sit on if I wanted to, or in whether there will be something which I can sit on when I want to (at the end of the walk). This interest will naturally lead to an interest in hearing the opinions of others as to where there are objects which I can sit on if I want to, irrespective of whether they want to sit on them or not; so I shall want them to operate an objectivised concept too. And if I grow a little more altruistic in my outlook I may even be interested in whether there is something which Fred can sit on if he wants to, irrespective of whether I shall want to sit on anything or not. Hence the concept of something which is, in abstraction from what any particular person wants at any particular time or place, or even from whether anyone ever wants to sit down, simply suitable for sitting on. It may right now be out of reach, it may be upside down, it may be folded up in a cardboard box, perhaps no-one will ever want to sit on it anyway; but it is a chair. I oversimplify, of course; there is more to the concept of a chair than that. Where a particular type of physical object is created to meet a need, physical characteristics as well as fitness for a certain purpose enter into the classification. But the simplification does not affect the point of the example, which is to illustrate the idea of the objectivisation of a concept, and at the same time to explain why we have objectivised concepts.

The explanation, we may note, is still of the 'state of nature' variety. It need not presuppose that the wholly egocentric, 'subjectivised' thought from which it began actually exists or existed, any more than a Hobbesian account of the State needs the corresponding presupposition about the war of every man against every man. The argument is only that if it exists, at any time, or in any individual, it will develop in the direction of objectivisation. Therefore there will be objectivised concepts, whether things started that way or not.

We can now apply these ideas to the situation of the inquirer and the concept of a good informant. We begin by considering it at its most subjective. I am seeking information as to whether or not p, and hence want an informant who is satisfactory for my purposes, here and now, with my present beliefs and capacities for receiving information. I am concerned, in other words, that as well as his having the right answer to my question,

(1) He should be accessible to me here and now.
(2) He should be recognisable by me as someone likely to be right about p.
(3) He should be as likely to be right about p as my concerns require.
(4) Channels of communication between him and me should be open.

There are various ways in which a candidate might fail these conditions. As regards the first, he might just not be here when I want him. Notice that in this context 'here' does not quite mean 'in the same place as I am'; it stretches to include all places which our systems of communication link with the place where I am. But at this stage we must also build in 'or soon can be'—for another subjectively varying factor will be the urgency of my situation; the less urgent, the laxer we can afford to be over the spatio-temporal requirements.

Equally, there are various ways of failing condition (2). One of them, of course, is by simply not being likely to be right about p. Another, if it is possible (I shall not try to resist those who feel that it isn't), is this: whilst being likely to be right about p, possessing no property whatever from which anyone, however knowledgeable and acute, could infer that one was likely to be right about it. Neither of these, clearly, have anything in particular to do with the state of our particular inquirer—if they hold, they hold for every inquirer—but there are many that do. For supposing that the candidate does possess a property which correlates well with being right about p, inquirers may (and mostly will) differ in point of their capacity to detect the property, and in point of knowledge of the correlation. One needs both of these to be able to detect the potential of the potential informant, so some inquirers will be better at it, some worse. Such differences may depend on sensory acuity, intellectual facility, theoretical background; they may also depend on altogether more transient features of inquirers, like their spatial position or bodily orientation. But all introduce a subjective element into the question: is Fred a good informant, for me, now, as to whether p?

Factor (3) gives a further dimension of subjectivity. The informant should be 'as likely to be right about p as my concerns require'. Take the inquirer, looking for a good informant as to whether p, in certain specific circumstances for certain specific purposes. We have seen that he will be interested in the candidate's competence not just in the actual world, but also in various possible worlds. Not, however, all worlds which strike him as theoretically possible, but only a selection of these. Some he will exclude because he has already come to believe that, although possible and even antecedently quite probable, they are not actual: he can see that the potential informant is wearing a red shirt, and so excludes those worlds in which he is wearing a blue shirt as merely possible and non-actual. In our earlier terminology, they are not 'open' possibilities for him any more.

Other possibilities he will exclude on slightly different grounds. Without actually taking them to be false he will regard them as so improbable that they need not be taken into account. So if the candidate would fail (hold the wrong belief as to whether p) in some world W, he will not allow that to influence his choice of informant if he puts the likelihood of W's being the actual world low enough. How low? That will depend on a number of factors. One is the urgency of forming a belief as to whether p, in the inquirer's particular situation: sometimes the penalty for not forming a belief at all (and so just dithering), is as great or greater than that for forming a false one. If my train leaves in 5 minutes I had better come to a decision about whether the station is this way or that way. Guessing will be better than not deciding, and anyone with a better than evens chance of telling me the right answer will be welcome. In such a storm, almost any port. (Had Descartes started on his meditations without first taking thought for his immediate practical needs, he could not have afforded to suspend virtually all belief on the chance of a *malin genie*—as he was well aware.) Another case concerns the relative pay-offs of being right and being wrong: if being wrong won't matter too much, but being right will be very advantageous, I may be satisfied with an informant of lower reliability, one whose views have a lower probability of being true, than I would be if the situation were reversed, so that being wrong would turn out very damaging. (The limiting case is surely Pascal's wager, where we are asked to adopt a belief without learning anything that raises the chances of its being true by any amount at all).[2] A further element is my personal attitude to risk. I may positively enjoy it, and so be prepared to take risks which I would not take if I enjoyed it less; one type of risk-taking is being somewhat less demanding in one's choice of informant. Or the converse: my natural inclination may be towards security. And all these calculations must be seen against the background of my circumstances. The rich aren't interested in winning small bets; for the poor a small stake can represent a big risk.

Lastly, there are many factors affecting fulfilment of condition (4), lying in various aspects of the relationship between inquirer and (potential) informant, and so liable to alter if either changes. Lack of a common language is one—for some values of p, though by no means all, it can often be overcome, by the use of gesture, for instance. Another is unwillingness to part with the information, something which, for a given informant, characteristically differs from one inquirer to another, and perhaps for the same inquirer from one time to another; that was the position of our gangster Luigi. Another concerns credibility—it can be that someone who clearly has an excellent chance of having a true belief about p is disqualified as an informant because there are reasons to doubt his sincerity; such was the position of Matilda, who told such dreadful lies that in the end no-one would believe her even when she was telling the truth—and this even though they could tell that her *belief* on the (may I say it?) burning question was almost certain to be the right one.

Whether I (subjectively) rate Fred a good informant depends in all these ways, and possibly a few more, on my situation and my relationship (in the broadest sense) to him. In pursuing my ends I must take them all into account. Others, who may be interested in Fred as a possible source of information, will not; they will have their own versions, arising out of their situation and their relationship to him.

What we have at this stage, then, is a number of individuals with the same problem—how to come by the truth as to whether p—and their various ways of approaching it, determined by their individual requirements and circumstances. But these individuals form a com-

[2] B. Pascal, para. 418.

munity, and are in some degree at least helpful to others and responsive to their needs. And even if I, as one of the community, am not so inclined, I shall still need an appreciation of their point of view if I am to be any good at getting them to help me. From such facts arises a pressure towards the formation of 'objectivised' concepts, concepts which separate as it were the common core from the multitude of accretions due to particular circumstances and particular persons and so varying with them.

To see how this may come about, consider that I shall hope that others will on occasion recommend informants to me. (This includes the case in which someone recommends himself.) I am not, of course, asking them to recommend people who, without their recommendation, would in any case have struck me as good informants. (This is one way in which my appreciation of their point of view comes in: if I am to be any judge of whom to ask for a recommendation, I shall need some idea of what sort of person might look like a good informant to them.) Quite the contrary: I want them to recommend as informants persons whom but for their help I could not have recognised. There are many detailed reasons why others may be in a position to do me such a service, but in general they come down to this: that they can detect properties of the informant which I cannot detect, or have more knowledge than I have of which properties correlate well with being right on the topic at issue. In practice this will mostly be a matter of their being 'better placed' than I am. As I seek to discover the close-of-play score there may be nothing about Fred to suggest to me that he would be a good person to ask. But Fred's friends are aware that he was at the ground when play finished; so their advice will help me. Amongst the best-placed observers of Fred is of course Fred himself—which is why people are so often in a good position, indeed often the best position, to advertise themselves as good informants.

As well as properties of Fred which I adventitiously cannot detect, there may be some which I am in general poor at detecting, and in the event of any of them correlating closely with Fred's capacity to form true beliefs on whatever it is I am curious about, I will hope that others, better endowed, will be prepared to point me towards Fred. In either case I am constructing the idea of someone who is a good informant, but whom for one reason or another I cannot detect as such. And I can go further, and conceive of someone who has a property correlating excellently with possession of the truth as to whether p, but which property no member of my community, or no member of my species, can detect.

Very similar considerations as those which apply to the correlating property also apply to the fact of the correlation. There may be many cases in which I can recognise the property X without difficulty, but not that possession of it correlates well with having the truth about p. Others may be better placed, and I shall hope for their goodwill and assistance. Again I can go further, and conceive of the case in which grasp of the correlation called for theoretical knowledge which nobody had, hence of somebody who might be discovered to have been a good informant but whom nobody could at present recognise as such. Perhaps I may go further still, and conceive of a correlation the recognition of which is not just beyond present human knowledge, but beyond human powers.

Some readers may feel that this kind of talk gives insufficient weight to verificationist lines of thought. But they shouldn't worry; nothing I have said here presupposes anything about verificationism, for or against. The suggestion was that someone might know something when we could not tell that he knew it. The verificationist warns us, on pain of insignificance, not to let that 'could not' become too strong. Let us agree, though without agreeing on any particular way of specifying the limits, and assign to 'could not' the maximum legitimate strength, whatever it may be. All I am trying to explain is how the process of 'objectivisation' of concepts might lead us to that thought, whatever it is.

It has to be said however that there is a good reason for the verificationist's discomfort that has nothing to do with verificationism. We are attempting a 'state of nature' explanation of a number of facts of conceptual or linguistic practice. Such explanations work by identifying certain human needs and arguing that the practices are a necessary (or at the least a highly appropriate) response to them; they will therefore be at their strongest when the human needs from which they start are the most practical, hence the most undeniable ones. This sets limits to what a 'state of nature' explanation can be good for. The less visible the practical significance, for us, of forming a certain conception or operating a certain linguistic usage, the weaker the explanation. Either it will become harder to mount a convincing argument that the needs we start from really do require the explanandum, or the less the needs will look like uncontroversial facts of the human condition. And if the visible practical significance sinks to zero, as one might think it had when we form the conception of a state of affairs which we are totally incapable of detecting, the force of a 'state of nature' explanation will sink to zero too, unless it takes the liberty of helping itself to additional explanatory principles. This is not to say, with the verificationist, that there is no such conception, only that a certain style of explanation is impotent to account for its existence, if it does exist.

But since for the moment we need only concern ourselves with covert and not with strictly undetectable properties we don't need to tread on any verificationist toes, or (what would worry me more) to go beyond the effective range of our method in order to use these thoughts about objectivisation for clarifying some of the problem cases. They indicate sufficiently why we will come to distinguish between the properties of the object which make it suitable for a certain use, and the properties of the user which make him capable of using it. To put it briefly: the two facts that human life is social, and that the members of a human society have differing capacities and perspectives, make it obligatory to form the separate conceptions of the state of the object, which is invariant with respect to different individuals, and the states of the 'consumers' of the object, which are not. We are in the same area here as are those ethical theorists who point out the social advantages of adopting moral principles which prescind from facts specific to individuals.

What happens to the concept at the centre of our investigation, that of the good informant, as objectivisation proceeds? The requirement of a true belief remains, and so does that of a property correlating well with truth of belief on the issue in hand, but that of the detectability of the property will be diluted. When we began the individual inquirer was looking for something that he could recognise there and then, preferably with a minimum of effort. That, of course, is what he will still hope for, but it is not what will be embodied in the public concept that now develops. For one thing, what is effortlessly available to him then and there will not be a matter of public interest, nor will it be the only thing that is of interest to him; for another, it will be in his interest to bear in mind the possibility of others having different (which will include more powerful) powers of detection, since that will at times be of use to him, let alone to them. The more we get used to the existence of such powers, the weaker will the detectability requirement, as reflected in the public concept, become. The concept of knowing, our hypothesis must now run, lies at the objectivised end of the process; we can explain why there is such an end, and why it should be found worth marking in language.

Earlier in this section we looked also at the third factor and the determinants of its most subjective versions, so to speak its 'me-here-now' shapes. How important is it to the particular inquirer, in his particular circumstances, to get the truth? What is his attitude towards risk? These are equally ripe for objectivisation. Just as I may have an interest in being able to sit down where and when I want to, without knowing exactly where or when that will be, so I may have an interest in collecting information while it is available, without knowing when, or why, or under what pressures, it may be needed. In addition, I shall be concerned—without knowing in detail what their circumstances and purposes are—that others should make judgements as to who is a good informant. That may be because I have enough altruism to wish that their enterprises in general, hence also their enterprises of belief-acquisition in particular, will succeed. But even without it I shall still want them to make assessments of informants, because that may turn out to be useful to me. I shall not suppose, however, that in making such assessments they have my particular circumstances in mind: if they tell me whom to ask about the times of trains to London, I shall not expect them to take into account how important it is to me to get the right answer, what I shall lose if I don't arrive on time. Perhaps I don't yet know that myself; perhaps it isn't even on my own behalf that I am trying to find out, but for someone else whose exact concern with the information is unknown to me.

All this is going to edge us towards the idea of someone who is a good informant as to whether p whatever the particular circumstances of the inquirer, whatever rewards and penalties hang over him and whatever his attitude to them. That means someone with a very high degree of reliability, someone who is very likely to be right—for he must be acceptable even to a very demanding inquirer. So of the worlds that we cannot quite definitely exclude, we shall want to include in our assessment of him even those that we regard as very improbable. Moreover, we shall be motivated to take a pretty careful look at those which we 'can quite definitely exclude'—is that really as many as we think? These thoughts take us further down the road of objectivisation. Knowledge, so the hypothesis goes, lies at the end of it.

My interest in other persons' powers of information-collection does not just arise from the fact that I may sometimes wish them to pass it on, or recommend informants to me. I shall become involved in group action, and affected by the actions of others; then circumstances will arise in which it is important to me that someone in the group holds a true belief as to whether p, and quite unimportant whether the route by which they acquired it would have been open to me or not. (I am very pleased that there are people who know how to disarm and dismantle a nuclear missile; but whether those who instructed them would also be prepared to instruct me is of no interest to me at all.) This throws light on cases in which condition (4) fails: that is to say in which a person is no good as an informant because the channels of communication are for some reason not open. Luigi and Matilda are both said to know, although hopeless as informants; he won't say, she won't be believed.

One way out of this difficulty would be to switch the hypothesis to the first-person case. If what we are concerned with are the circumstances under which we take ourselves as informants, so to speak—when we decide that one of our own beliefs is reliable—then problems about channels of communication will not enter into it, since they may be assumed always to be open. But although there may be something in this (I certainly don't want to deny that first-personal considerations may have a role to play in shaping the concept) it would be feeble to make it the main plank of our explanation. Concern about the truth of one's own beliefs calls for some theoretical sophistication, and although I would hazard a guess—it is not so very hazardous, when one comes to think of it—that it is a degree of sophistication that exists wherever language, and the concept of knowledge, are found, it is still preferable to keep the basis of our investigation as primitive as possible, which means sticking to the third-person approach unless absolutely forced to abandon it.

Whether that point will ever come or not, we haven't reached it yet. Just as properties of the potential informant are not simply detectable or undetectable, but detectable for some under certain circumstances and undetectable for others, or under other circumstances, so the question whether channels of communication are open or not isn't a simple Yes or No matter, but depends on facts about the particular inquirer and his relationship to the possible informant. Luigi won't tell me what happened to Mario, but he may tell Carlo. Now the objection may be made here that unless

Carlo is prepared to spill the beans (which he isn't, unless Luigi is a very bad judge of whom it is safe to talk to), that won't make much difference to me—so we still don't have an account of why I should be motivated to form the objectivised concept which applies to Luigi although he won't tell me. True, but not all examples are like that. My student won't tell me what is worrying him, but perhaps he will tell someone at the university counselling service, and then (whether the news is passed on to me or not) something may get done that will help—and incidentally that will make my life easier as well as his. It will surely be to my disadvantage if I don't have the conceptual resources to recognise the visiting Chinese delegates as a source of information just because there is a blockage in the linguistic pipeline. After all, they will happily tell the interpreter, and the interpreter will tell me.

Some philosophers, on thinking of this type of prima facie counter-example to the hypothesis that knowing is being a good informant, will say at once that knowing seems to be that central state of the subject which fits him to be a good informant, other circumstances concurring. It isn't, on my view, that they are wrong. My criticism, if that be the right word, is just that it would be more satisfying to have some explanation of how and why such a concept comes to be formed. That is what the idea of objectivisation provides. But there is another point to be noticed: the concept thus explained is not quite captured by the above form of words. The words were, 'that central state of the subject which fits him to be a good informant, other circumstances concurring', and one natural way of reading them is a long way from the concept of knowledge.

We have seen that, if other circumstances concur, someone with only a fairly good chance of being right may be perfectly acceptable as an informant. Perhaps no-one more likely to be right exists, the prize for holding (and following) the right opinion is high, the penalty for following the wrong one is trivial. But that informant is not rated as knowing. For that an informant needs a very good chance of being right, so that the concept we are looking for is more like that of being in a state which makes him a good informant about *p whether other circumstances concur or not*. Such is the position when we consider condition (3), but we find just the reverse if we focus on condition (2). In respect of condition (2) nobody is ever a good informant unless circumstances concur—if they don't, even the most obvious of correlating properties may be unrecognisable, or unrecognisable as such, and the information-potential go begging.

Is this asymmetry damaging to our thesis? I think not. The thesis brings with it no commitment to the view that the objectivisation of each of the features (1) to (4) (plus any others there may be) proceeds in the same way, or in such a way that some simple verbal formula can be found that neatly fits them all. It demands only that what happens in each case be readily understandable in terms of motivations which our hypothesis suggests; and about this there is no great difficulty. In saying that someone knows whether p we are certifying him as an informant on that question, and we have no idea of the practical needs of the many people who may want to take him up on it; hence a practice develops of setting the standard very high, so that whatever turns, for them, on getting the truth about p, we need not fear reproach if they follow our recommendation. (Where, as in the murder trial, we positively know that the most serious consequences turn on it, our inclination is to wind the standard up yet another notch.) Condition (2), the accessibility of the correlating property, plays a very different role. In recommending an informant to you I am indeed implying that the likelihood of his being right is as great as your concerns require; but I am not implying that the facts that signal that likelihood are accessible to your cognitive equipment. Indeed, it is just when they are not that you most stand in need of my recommendation.

The point turns on a 1st/3rd person asymmetry. The inquirer can make use of another's identification of the good informant, but he must act on the information, when it comes, himself. So when I identify a good informant on your behalf I need not bother myself with the question whether you could, in principle, have made the identification yourself—it just doesn't matter. But I do have to bother whether the reliability of the informant meets your standards, since it is you who will act on the information; therefore, if I don't know what you want it for or what fate awaits you if you get it wrong, I had better make sure that the level of reliability is very high indeed.

Some readers, I anticipate, will have got the feeling that the cart is before the horse. Don't you need to know first, before qualifying as an informant? Shouldn't being a good informant be explained in terms of knowing whether p, rather than the other way round? The reaction is obviously a natural one, and more than that, there is a good deal of force in it.

We are going to have to accept that the relationship, if it exists, is between knowing and having potential as an informant—we have seen that someone may be a perfectly good knower when, for one reason or another, the channels of communication are closed or malfunctioning. And this may be taken to suggest that being a good informant is knowing plus some other factor (communication, credibility); and this in turn to mean that knowing is primary, being a good informant derivative, contrary to my approach.

Nevertheless there are, compatible with this admission, two ways of looking at the relationship between knowledge and capacity qua informant. One would be to say that the former is in fact best understood without reference to the notion of value as an informant, and that the latter then arises out of it as a welcome social bonus. That line is indeed incompatible with my project, but there is another which is not: that knowing is best understood in terms of the idea of a potential informant, that we get at its nature by first considering the business of being a good informant and then subtracting something from the result, or modifying it in some way. The concept of the informant will then leave its mark, so to speak, on the concept of knowledge, and the hypothesis is that for this reason an approach via the former concept will be likely to provide a more illuminating account of the concept of knowledge than will any other method.

It may improve the reader's grasp of this point, as well as perhaps raising his estimation of its prospects, to return to an example which has served us earlier in this section. Consider the imaginary case of someone interested in the concept of a chair, who observes that most of us like to sit down, and suggests that the concept of a chair arises as part of our response to this need; this, he urges, is likely to prove a particularly illuminating approach. Thereupon a dissenting voice is heard, warning us that we are in danger of getting the cart before the horse. Surely we can see (thus the voice) that things that are not in position to satisfy the need to sit down can perfectly well be chairs. If I need to sit down, only something which is then within my reach can satisfy the need; a chair dropped off by some expedition in the middle of the Sahara can't satisfy anyone's need (there's no one within 200 miles of it, let us say); something might be a chair although it could only be used by a young child; a chair on top of a bonfire that is already blazing is still a chair. So (still the dissenting voice speaking) don't try to explain what a chair is by reference to the satisfaction of the need to sit; first tell us what a chair is, then it will be clear that, and why, chairs are good for sitting on—provided they are in the right place, and of the right size, and the right stability, relative to the prospective sitter.

I offer this as a prima facie parallel to the objection that, since one can easily think of cases in which a knower may not be a good informant (because something or other is blocking the channel of communication) we should not give priority to the latter idea in giving an account of the former. If it is parallel, then obviously hope remains; for most will agree that the dissenting voice of the previous paragraph has got things wrong somehow; and if it has, then maybe the comparable objection in the case of the concept of knowledge is in the same boat. One would not find out much about why there are chairs, or why the concept of a chair has the boundaries (fuzzy though they be) that it has, by concentrating attention on the shape and constitution of the things to the exclusion of what they were for. To be lead into that state of mind by the observation that some chairs, for one reason or another, cannot be sat on, would be a heuristic disaster. A chance has to be given to the hypothesis that the same is true of knowledge, and the objection equally misconceived.

To show that it certainly is misconceived would be to show that the project of this essay, indeed the particular hypothesis under consideration, certainly succeeds, and that may be asking too much. But we can fairly quickly say enough to show that we are perfectly justified in proceeding, and that the 'cart before the horse' objection shouldn't be allowed to bring the investigation to a halt. In the first place, we imagine, the members of any society will be interested in obtaining information from their fellows, and to this end they will develop a concept very like our concept of a good informant—one who (predictably) believes the truth on a given matter, and is prepared, and available, to pass his opinion on comprehensibly and without dissembling. The process of the objectivisation of concepts which may be thought of as having started out in much more heavily subjective versions has already been described in outline. It will lead to a concept which so far as possible leaves out of account those features of the original concept that fitted it for the particular use of the person applying it, with his particular location, powers of discernment and comprehension, relationship to the potential informant, and so on. What remains will not be identifiable with the concept of a good informant—as indeed we have already seen that there are many knowers who for one reason or another are not good informants; but it may still bear certain marks of its origin, and if it does then the concept of the good informant may be the key for drawing them to our attention and making their presence comprehensible to us. It will also bear the marks of the objectivisation. Some of the marks may obscure some of the others.

By envisaging such a story we do several things which the proponent of the 'cart before the horse' objection does not. If we say: 'Knowledge first, and then comes the capacity to inform', we leave it obscure why the concept of knowledge should ever have arisen, rather as the comparable objection about the concept of a chair would leave that concept, and even more so the chairs themselves, unaccountable brute-fact bits of the mental and physical habitats. Of course the objector may (in the case of knowledge, scarcely in that of chairs) go on to make a positive contribution in the shape of some alternative hypothesis. Then we have—what the cart-before-the-horse objection by itself does not give us—an honest confrontation, which is to be decided, if at all, in the way in which such confrontations are usually and properly decided: by weighing the plausibility of the opposing views, the amount of detailed fact which each can explain, the elegance and accuracy with which it explains it.

Taken on its own without the support of any alternative hypothesis the objection does not therefore have much force. Nor does it suggest any further lines of inquiry or explanatory possibilities, whereas this is precisely what my theory does. As well as offering a plausible account of the purpose of the concept, it introduces the notions of the good informant, and of conceptual objectivisation, and these may have other uses besides those we have so far seen. Objectivisation, for instance, may help us understand the phenomenon of scepticism. But that is a large topic, and deserves a section of its own.

XI

In the preceding section one of the questions we considered was how the third condition (that the candidate-informant be 'as likely to be right about p as my concerns require') will fare as objectivisation proceeds. What we saw was that there will be a shift towards adopting a high value for the likelihood required before we are willing to recommend an informant. For the conditions under which we recommend informants will not, in general, be ones in which the recommender is sufficiently aware of the concerns for which the informant and his information are needed. This fact will push the required standard up to such a level that the recommender may responsibly issue his recommendation whilst knowing nothing of them, that is to say, to a level which the recommender may reasonably take to be high enough to satisfy all, or all practical, purposes. Our use of 'knows', so says the hypothesis, marks the attainment of that level. On the other hand, it would be most disadvantageous if we were unwilling to offer any information except when we took that level to be reached; so for lower levels we have more guarded forms of words available: 'I'm pretty sure that . . .', 'He's usually a good judge of this sort of thing', and many others.

Is there anything more we can say as to just what level this is? The above line of argument would suggest a fairly stark answer: the probability that the belief is true needs to be 1, no less. For if it is less that 1, can we not imagine an inquirer whose concerns, whose game-theoretic situation, are such that that likelihood of truth is insufficient for him rationally to commit himself, and consequently also insufficient for another responsibly to commit himself on his behalf?

Important here, however, is the word 'imagine'. As the probability approaches 1 it becomes progressively easier to imagine such an inquirer than to identify one. And what one encounters only in the imagination—if indeed one's imagination runs to it at all—has very much less influence in determining the shape of an everyday conceptual practice than what a community actually encounters in its living experience. If we are forced to put a precise numerical value on an acceptable probability-coefficient, it may well be that it can only be 1. But if we are forced to do that it is we who are forcing ourselves. The subject matter does not demand it, or even encourage it; we are talking of an all but universal everyday practice, and everyday thinking about likelihoods does not go on in such precise quantitative terms; it is far too like a feeling for that. What we should do here is look to imprecisely quantified concepts like 'being sure' and 'feeling certain' or (with a eye to Austin's treatment of the topic)[1] to that of offering a guarantee, or promise, of truth. All of these, as the detail of recent debate bears witness, have a role in our more or less untutored reactions to questions about the concept of knowledge, and it is to help us to see why that is so that these thoughts about objectivisation are appropriately employed—not to generate spuriously mathematicised probability statements.

It is now the moment to break down the fence I may be thought to have been by implication erecting around 'everyday' practice, apparently isolating it from non-everyday practices which involve, and are in part the outcome of, reflective thought. We have no clear grasp of such a distinction, any more than we have of the distinction one sometimes hears of between philosophical and non- or pre-philosophical thinking. But even though the fence is to be taken down, it has served a methodological point. A recurring theme has been the universality of the practice we are investigating, and the way in which this demands an explanation in terms of conditions which hold just as universally, that is, in every community that operates a language. That requires, not that we fence off practice from reflection, since there may be some kinds of reflection which can with great plausibility be argued to be just as universal, just as much demanded by the state of nature as it affects beings of human intelligence, as the particular linguistic or conceptual phenomenon we are trying to account for; if so, those kinds of reflection have a perfectly good place in the account. The distinction we should be aware of is the one between those and the kind of reflection that is a response to conditions which, although they may be wide-spread in certain places at certain times in history, or amongst certain

---

[1] J. L. Austin, pp. 67–9.

types of people, cannot with the same conviction be thought to hold with scarcely an exception.

Two such conditions certainly have an effect upon our concept of knowledge as soon as we begin to reflect on them, and they are found, I would hazard the guess, in every society that we would think of as civilised or advanced, as well as many that we wouldn't. One is the practice of betting on outcomes at quantified rates, so that potential winnings are roughly proportioned to the judged unlikelihood of the outcome; a lottery, in which the chances of winning decrease in exact proportion to the number of entrants, and the jackpot increases in the same proportion with the increased number of stakes, is a precisely quantifiable (though doubtless less widespread) form of such a wager. The second practice is a sophisticated inferential one: that of drawing conclusions that depend upon a large number of premises.

What the example of a lottery does is to bring much closer to our real experience the idea of someone who would not necessarily be well advised to accept information which had a chance less than 1 of being right. Consider the claim that this particular ticket, the one he is about to buy, will not win. We can make the likelihood that this claim is correct as high as we like, short of 1, by enlarging the number of tickets going into the draw. But since by enlarging the total number of tickets we also proportionately increase the prize without increasing the stake, it may make perfectly good sense for our punter, especially if the cost of a ticket is trivial to him, to reject the information that this one will not win and go ahead and buy it. Only if he believes the probability to be 1 can it be clear that he should take the informant to be good enough for his purposes.

The same sort of practical considerations as were at work in the less precisely quantifiable cases are at work in the case of the large lottery, and it can be seen how they push our estimate of the probability that will 'do' up to 1, or certainty. So the idea that someone only knows whether p if something about the situation makes it certain that their belief on that question is right has some basis in the practical, even if it is not a basis that we can expect strictly everyone to encounter. A similar push is exerted by the wish to draw inferences from multiple premises and be able to rely on the result.

The point is well-known, as is the fact that the example of the lottery can be mobilised again to illustrate it. If

I know that a, I know that b, ... I know that n

is to legitimise my claim to know anything that I know to follow from the conjunction (*a* & *b* & ... & *n*), and if this is to hold for arbitrarily long conjunctions, then I can only claim knowledge of propositions whose probability I can set at 1. For suppose I allow that there can be knowledge that *p* so long as the probability of *p*'s falsehood is below $1/n$, I only have to think of a lottery with more than *n* tickets to be able to say of each ticket that I know that it will not win. And then, if we suppose that I also know that those are all the tickets, the conjunctive principle allows me knowledge that no ticket will win, something which, on the contrary, I actually know to be false.

The wish to be able to rely on the conclusion of an essentially many-premised inference isn't unique to gamblers, or to citizens of the scientifically more advanced societies. Consider the chieftain of a tribe who wonders whether he knows that no member of his army would betray their plans to the neighbouring enemy. On the basis of report and personal acquaintance he feels sure, for each one, that *he* would not do it. Does he, mindful of his responsibility for the tribe's security, now conclude that he knows that nobody would do it, and take no further precautions against treachery? He will be keenly aware that he only needs to be wrong in one case out of, perhaps, several hundred. Such situations automatically raise the stakes, force up the demands on what, for these purposes, is usable information and an acceptable informant.

Lotteries, of course, have another feature which this situation does not. They have winners; or at least the participants believe them to have winners, and would not participate otherwise. So when we think of the possibility of winning a big lottery we are not (as we see it) thinking of something that just might happen: the minute chance of winning, we believe, always comes good for someone or other. And if we are reflective enough to compare their epistemic position before the draw with our own and everybody else's we find, assuming that we believe the draw to have been fair, no relevant difference. Someone who told them that they would not win would have been wrong; someone who told us that we would not win would have been right, but could not have been reliable.

Our chieftain is not in quite the same position. He does not have to face the fact that every army has its enemy agent—it doesn't. But he may well believe, indeed know, that some well-screened organisations have turned out to harbour traitors, and if he is wise he must allow this to affect his attitude to his present information.

What we see from all this is how factors arising out of special, but not for that reason extremely rare, conditions, given a little reflection of no very high-brow kind, force up our estimate of the level of likelihood required. Two things are to be noted at this point:

To find a need to raise the likelihood to 1 takes a little extrapolative imagination. Real situations sometimes force us to set it very high indeed, but not actually at 1. Perhaps because of that, the final push towards a probability of 1 only makes itself felt in circumstances which invite reflection. In everyday practice we happily bandy the word 'know' about without having to feel that our chances of being wrong are literally zero—and this is in good accord with my genetic account of the concept and pragmatic account of its point.

Secondly, even when we do set the likelihood at 1 that does not mean the type of absolute certainty, invulnerability to literally any theoretical possibility, which the sceptic characteristically demands and finds us unable to provide. Nothing about our reactions to lotteries or the danger of treachery need push us any further than the demand that the actual or 'real' chance of being wrong should be zero. Hence, I suggest, the attractiveness of the idea that someone knows whether p when something about him is connected as a matter of natural law with his holding the right belief about p.[2] Such an analysis, one can now see, has a rightful place in the debate. But one can also see that mistakes may have been made about what that place is, in particular when it has been announced as the analysis of the concept of knowledge. What it is, rather, is a reflective tidy-up of everyday practice—and indeed a well-founded tidy-up, since it emerges very naturally from the motivation which gave rise to the practice in the first place. But it also needs to be said that it is, as tidy-ups go, pretty disruptive. For if we were really to conform our practice to its recommendations we would have to be either very cautious, or very trusting, in our ascriptions of knowledge. Whether we really know enough about the states of subjects and the laws in accordance with which the mind forms beliefs, ever to be in a position to say that some belief of Fred's will be true as a matter of natural law, must be open to serious doubt—remember

[2] e.g. D. M. Armstrong, esp. pp. 166 ff.

that we would need to know this *before* knowing whether the belief in question was true or not, so a straight appeal to natural determinism (supposing we knew it to hold) is of no avail. Indeed we may already know enough about the complexity of the brain and the role which its complexities play in belief-formation to decide here and now that we will never be able to say that since Fred is in such-and-such a state his belief as to whether p will be true as a matter of natural law.

XII

The first step in writing about scepticism must be to say what one is writing about. A negative attitude towards almost any generally received truth can be called scepticism, and in the course of the history of thought a wide variety of positions have been so called. Certain ancient sceptics were known to recommend abrogation of all belief in furtherance of inner peace. Hume, for many a paradigm sceptic, regarded such a recommendation as potentially disastrous, but happily impossible to follow. His scepticism consisted primarily in a drastic re-evaluation of the powers of reason to underpin belief. In the twentieth century the sceptic has mostly been thought of as someone who denies that we know anything much; how close to Hume he may be depends on Hume's concept of reason and its relation to this sceptic's concept of knowledge.

In offering to show how the existence of a debate about scepticism is a product of the concept of knowledge, I do not of course have anything like this range of material in mind. That all the positions commonly called scepticism form an intellectual natural kind, about which one can aspire to generalise without falling into triviality, is unlikely almost beyond consideration. What I shall try to do is to account for the role played in this debate by a certain type of argument, familiar to every student of philosophy from the first of Descartes's *Meditations*, where it is exemplified by the thought of the deceitful demon. The strategy is to invent a hypothesis with two properties: first, it would make no noticeable difference for us if it were true; secondly, if it were true virtually all our present beliefs would be false. Then it is urged that, because of the second property, we must either show that the hypothesis is not true or abandon virtually all claims to knowledge; and that because of the first property we cannot show that it is not true. Nowadays the demon has a colleague in the scientist whose computer feeds perfectly 'normal' stimulation to an excised brain floating in nutrient fluid. Technology has advanced but the problem remains the same: how to exclude the possibility that I am such a brain, how to claim any knowledge of my environment if I cannot?

This style of argument fascinates, which is why we find so many attempts to reply to it. But at the same time there is a feeling of unreality about it, which is why so many of the attempts begin in a posture of condescension, with the assumption that it must be mistaken. Some, like Moore's famous response,[1] very nearly end there. But still the feeling persists that there is a problem. Nozick presented it as a major advantage of his analysis of knowledge that it disposed of just this type of sceptical argument; in this he was quite mistaken,[2] but the point remains that in 1981 he regarded the job as still eminently worth doing. What I hope to explain is the existence of both of these opposed reactions, and the apparent difficulty of bringing about a decision between them. Up to now I have been trying to account for features philosophers have discerned in the content of the everyday concept of knowledge; now I consider something that characteristically happens when philosophers talk about its range of application.

That way of putting the matter presupposes that there is some connection here, that the everyday conceptual practice is at least to some extent influential in shaping the philosophical debate. One hypothesis, which by implication I have put forward elsewhere,[3] suggests a different sort of explanation. A philosopher may work under the influence of a picture of the nature of reality and of man which assigns special status to a particular kind of relationship between the human mind and the objects of its thought. And this may incline him to reserve the honorific word 'knowledge' for that kind of relationship, and so to deny that most of what ordinarily passes for knowledge 'really' is such. In recommending his ideal to us, he recommends a change of usage. (Conversely, his change of usage is not arbitrary: it expresses his ideal.) And it is perfectly possible that even his opponents may accept his usage, his way of thinking of knowledge, and do so precisely for the purpose of showing his ideal to be beyond realisation. If they do, they will end up saying that there is no knowledge, or very little. What they thereby reject, however, is not the everyday practice involving 'know' and its cognates, but the cognitive ideal associated with this

---

[1] See G. E. Moore.   [2] See E. J. Craig, (3).
[3] See E. J. Craig, (2), esp. chs. 1 and 2.

particular *Weltbild*, perhaps thereby the whole *Weltbild* as well. It is not clear that the everyday practice is playing a formative part in this debate at all; perhaps it is doing no more than lending it a word.

One reply here, as usual, would be 'the proof of the pudding': does it turn out, on inspection, that the same hypothesis that accounts for so many of the facts about the everyday practice also serves us well in understanding the status of the traditional sceptical fantasies? But even before we start tasting the pudding there is reason to think that not everything can depend in this way on the background metaphysic.

Someone who thinks that the background metaphysic is all there is to it will surely be at a loss to explain the intuitive impact of the Cartesian strategy. On this view the strategy is simply a covert way of urging us to adopt different standards, those enthroned by the ideal, and then show that these standards are hardly ever met; it is not an attempt to convince us that hardly anything reaches the standards we now set, therefore it poses no challenge to anything we presently believe. If there were something else behind it, namely the idea that the 'new' standards really are the ones we now set, if only we would examine them carefully, or that they emerge from the ones we now set as an obviously natural extension; if something of this kind were in the offing, then that would be a different matter, and might well induce the feeling that we were up against a sceptical threat. That however would call for a rather different explanation, one giving an account not just of the motivation for the philosopher's standards, but also of the features of the everyday concept of knowledge (or whatever) which linked it to them.

What this means is that we have to look at another type of hypothesis, one which finds seeds of scepticism in the everyday concept itself, prior to any philosophical modification. It is not, as I have in effect just said, at odds with a hypothesis of the former kind, but complementary to it. For if a philosopher bends the concept of knowledge to make it fit for duty at a particular station in his system, one fact we should not forget is that it was that concept which he elected to bend, rather than another, or rather than delimiting a new concept and inventing a word for it; and there may be something in the nature of the everyday concept that made it a specially suitable choice. There may be, in other words, some feature of the everyday concept which generates pressure towards

scepticism, or opportunities for it, and there might be something
in our philosopher's metaphysic or *Weltbild* which inclined him
to emphasise that feature. These remarks are obscure, partly because
anticipatory, but I hope they sufficiently indicate that we need not
think of the two styles of explanation as mutually exclusive.

Before trying to explain anything we had better pause for a longer
look at the facts to be explained; when we do it appears that what
we are looking for must involve (at least) two complementary components. For the reasons given above it can hardly be the case that
the explanation lies wholly insulated from everyday practice,
depending solely on the properties of various thought-structures
in which only a tiny fragment of humanity have ever taken any
interest. That would make it look too much like an accident that
scepticism tends to be expressed in terms of the words 'know' and
'knowledge'. Besides that, there is the fact that when it is proposed
to us—meaning any of us who are prepared to think about such
things—that we hardly know anything unless we can rule out the
possibility of the demon, our reaction is not the same as it would
be if we were told that there aren't any doctors unless there is
someone who can cure any disease within two minutes.[4] Most
of us don't much like the former point, but we find it all a bit
puzzling and, partly for that reason, irritating; the latter is just mani-
festly fatuous and arbitrary. Evidently the sceptical argument con-
nects in some way with something or other from the conceptual
practice that we all naturally grow up into.

On the other hand, it would surely be misplaced to want the
explanation of the existence of that conceptual practice to lead
straight into an explanation of the impact of the Cartesian argument
without any additional input. For in that event the question whether
anyone knows anything much, and divergence about the way to
answer it, would be a part of the everyday scene—which it isn't.
So to account for its presence in philosophy we need either a further
factor not a part of every community's mental life, or another feature
of the everyday which inhibits it. And in the second case we should
still want to know what it may be in some philosophers that conquers
the inhibition. What is wanted, given the explanatory tools I am
employing, is an account of the likely genesis of features of the
everyday practice which offer handholds both to persons motivated

[4] I borrow the example, though not the use of it, from Paul Edwards.

towards scepticism and to persons motivated away from it. Preferably, they should not be such as to award victory to either; for
if they were, one or the other would long ago have won.

A last preliminary point: some may think that the restriction to
the argument from demons and brains in vats robs my enterprise
of most of its promised significance. There are so many other routes,
it may be said, to radical scepticism. My reply, for which I shall
offer some reasons in Section XIII, would be: perhaps, but not as
many as has been suggested. If we understood the attraction and
repulsion of the sceptical strategy of Descartes's first *Meditation*,
we would have gone a long way.

In Section X we looked at the phenomenon of objectivisation
and the way it will act to transform the inquirer's original, subjectively relativised notion of a good informant. Of the four factors
we considered, numbers (1), (2), and (4) do not, so far as I can
see, have anything to do with scepticism or any tendency to scepticism latent in the concept of knowledge. But what may well have
something to do with scepticism is condition (3): that the informant
should be as likely to be right about *p* as the subject's present concerns require.

What we saw was that the objectivisation of this notion will tend
to push up the standards demanded of the informant's reliability.[5]
When we collect information, seek informants, or recommend
informants to others, we invariably do so in a state of extensive
ignorance; amongst the things we are very often, if not absolutely
always, ignorant about are the purposes for which the information
will be used, by whom, and under what conditions. That is to say,
we are ignorant of just those factors which determine the acceptable
levels of reliability in the wholly subjective case. We therefore adopt
a strategy designed to succeed whatever—the same response as orig-
inally introduced counterfactuality into the concept of knowledge—
in this case: set a standard high enough to face the worst with.
Then we have vocabulary, and a style of speech (remember that
someone can in effect claim knowledge of something without mentioning the word 'know', merely by the way they announce it) which
marks this standard, and more cautious forms for offering information of lesser reliability. The possibility of the worst compels
observance of the highest standard, and this is what the concept

---

[5] See also Section XI.

of knowledge certifies.

As the reader will have recognised, I am now in danger of making things much too easy for myself, for what these superlatives ('worst' and 'highest') mean is still unclear, and they may mislead. The danger is of slipping into saying that for knowledge, given that the concept is governed by objectivisation in the way just envisaged, 'absolute' objectivisation is called for, meaning by that the demand that the informant be certain to have the right answer in any conceivable world, including those 'sceptical worlds' of demons and brains in vats; that the 'highest' standard, in other words, means a standard capable of withstanding any conceivable mishap. That would explain how and why the concept of knowledge brings scepticism in its train; but of course it is not within a mile of being warranted by anything we have established so far. It is rather as if we had said, with Peter Unger,[6] that knowing (given its genesis) will come out as 'being right as to whether p, and not by accident', and then assumed permission to say that someone who is right, but would be wrong if he were a brain in a vat, or a victim of the demon, is only right to some degree by accident—leaving ourselves just as open to the charge of misusing the notion of an accident as the sceptic is to misusing that of knowledge. Perhaps he doesn't misuse it, and perhaps this would not be a misuse of the concept of the accidental—but on that issue this cheap manœuvre does not advance understanding one inch. The hypothesis was that knowledge 'lies at the end of the road of objectivisation', but where does that road come to an end, or when have we gone far enough? The whole issue turns on finding a justified answer to that question.

It should be said straight away that Unger's spectacular and notorious argument for scepticism[7] did not involve the cheap and question-begging manœuvre, but rather made use of a far subtler thought. He began by pointing out a category of what he called 'absolute terms'. Being flat, he said, means being perfectly flat—not *at all* bumpy—a standard which, for all we know, quite likely nothing whatever achieves, but which in all practical contexts is relaxed in accordance with the degree of flatness needed for whatever purposes are under consideration—a rugby pitch, a lawn, a billiard table. A necessary condition of knowing, he then argued, is being certain.

---

[6] See P. Unger, (1).   [7] See P. Unger, (2) and (3).

And 'certain' is an absolute term: being certain is being absolutely certain, as being flat is being absolutely flat, and being a vacuum is being absolutely empty. So we should consider 'know' in the same light: we may and do relax the standard, but the standard calls for the truth of the belief to be (absolutely) certain, so it is truly satisfied only by a belief whose truth would survive even the worst efforts of the demon. At most hardly any surfaces are flat, and hardly any of the regions we declare to be vacua actually are such; so in respect of both these terms we say a lot of things which are false, but they are usually close enough to being true for their falsity to have no adverse practical effects, given the purposes we have in mind. Our claims to knowledge, Unger holds, are in the same position. The sceptic is therefore right, though the point that he typically insists on, that we do not know anything, makes no significant practical difference.

It may look as if Unger's view would explain both the existence of scepticism (which results from the perception of its truth) and the resistance to it (which is a mistaken reaction to its practical insignificance). His view is equivalent to the thought, expressed in our terminology, that the objectivisation which forms the concept of knowledge goes to the very limit of theoretical possibility. Every conceivable way in which the belief that p could be wrong—and in the hardline version perhaps also all the inconceivable ways—has to be taken into consideration. Since Unger's arguments for ascribing such a sense to 'know', though far from negligible, do not wholly convince me (nor, as we shall see, do they nowadays wholly convince Unger), I would be more at ease with their conclusion if I could see some practical motive which might push the process of objectivisation to the theoretical limit in the way it implies.

Finding such a motive is not going to be easy. There is nothing new in the point that human life takes place against a background of beliefs, assumptions, presuppositions, or whatever we wish to call them. That we are brains in vats, or victims of a Cartesian demon, or that the deity is about to revise all the laws of nature, these are thoughts we can just about entertain—with a bit of practice. But it took a highly unusual thinker, conducting a highly unusual investigation, to suggest them to us in the first place, and when they are suggested our mind in a sense rules them out at once. Nor is it surprising that nature should operate some kind of automatic defences against thoughts which, taken seriously, could only paralyse our powers of decision and action. That isn't yet to say, as some opponents of scepticism have said, that they belong to the pathological side of our mental life; but it is to say that they have a role in it only under very special circumstances, which certainly don't include the ordinary social practice of gathering and passing on information, or certifying informants. In deciding whether Fred can be advanced as an acceptable informant as to whether p nobody considers whether he would answer correctly were he (or they) subject to some systematic Cartesian illusion and then, having decided that he would not, tries to calculate how much damage the fact does to his credentials by asking how likely it is that that 'possibility' will be realised. Just as importantly, nobody, however vital to them it is that they get at the truth about p, expects anyone else to consider such matters before recommending an informant; nor does anybody consider them before relying on one of their own beliefs. Unger himself makes a remark which only sharpens the difficulty:

... with respect to the matter of whether there are elephants, for practical purposes there is no important difference between whether you know that there are elephants or whether you are in that position with respect to the matter that you actually are in.[8]

Why do we have the absolute concept of knowledge, must we not ask, rather than the concept of this other state (the one we 'actually are in'), or some vaguer concept taking in both, if 'for practical reasons there is no important difference' between the circumstances in which they apply? Or how do we arrive at it if the thoughts it embraces (such as those of the classical sceptical possibilities) have no role whatever in everyday mental life? The reply might be made that even if we cannot answer those questions we can still point to various 'absolute' concepts which uncontroversially have been formed—so there is no insuperable difficulty about their formation, even if we do not see how it can happen. But this takes us only half way, for in the case of knowledge there is a problem which is not nearly so acute when we are thinking of emptiness or flatness.

I do not want to insist that 'flat' and 'empty' definitely are absolute terms in Unger's sense. But if they are, as is on first impression quite plausible, at least one can think of (reasonably) everyday processes of thought which might have made them that way. Notice that whatever processes our explanation calls upon do have to be

[8] Ibid., (2), p. 201.

classifiable, without too painful a stretch, as 'everyday'; we are deal-ing here with a thesis about *the* concepts of knowledge, flatness and such, not with concepts that occur only in the work of certain particular thinkers, presumably as a result of some thoughts or needs peculiar to a very few. What is under investigation is equipment supposed to be known and used by more or less everyone.

From this point of view, the immediately striking thing about 'flat' and 'empty' is that they have to do with series that are felt to be seamlessly continuous. Once we have the idea of the contents getting less, the bumps getting lower, the mind can hardly help passing to the thoughts of even less, and lower still. And there is no reason to stop where unaided perception gives out, nor would there be even if it gave out at the same point for all of us. For one thing, something which is perfectly flat to visual and tactual inspection may turn out not to be flat enough for our purposes when we try to use it as a snooker table, or as a mirror. And for another, the images of things not available to unaided perception which are made available by microscopy or a simple magnifying glass are very like unmagnified images of familiar sized, ordinarily bumpy objects. If we try to imagine what a surface which to us appears flat is like for a very minute creature with perceptual acuity suitable to the size of its body, we may very well use the same imagery as we would use in imagining ourselves in a jagged, broken landscape.

The ways in which a belief can fail to be knowledge, however, do not hang together in the same way. There is here no ordered series of items or states of the same kind being successively revealed by continuous improvement of some kind of intellectual sensitivity. One could indeed speak in these terms of the passage from everyday mistakes to the wholesale error induced by the demon, but it would be a metaphor comprehensible only to someone who already knew the literature of scepticism. The imagination is not lead smoothly on in the same way from case to case. Without special circumstances, or special prompting, I see no reason why it should ever make the transition.

There is a problem, therefore, as to how the concept of knowledge could have arisen, given Unger's account of it. But there is another and sharper problem: why should scepticism have met with such resistance? Consider the term 'vacuum', to which 'knowledge' is alleged to be analogous. What would be the likely response to the suggestion that scarcely any of the things we refer to as 'a vacuum' actually is such? Surely the response, after a little havering perhaps, would be that it is quite true: 'vacuum' picks out as it were an 'ideal' state to which the best of our vacua are good approximations— and that what approximations count as good depends on which purposes the so-called vacuum is to serve. (And one might well add that although the suggestion is quite true, there are not many situations in which one would be doing anything more than making a nuisance of oneself by insisting on it.) But a debate, with each of two or more parties warmly advocating their own view, one would not expect; and it is not in fact found. 'Are there nearly as many vacua as we commonly think?' isn't an issue, and this is reflected in the fact that many would prefer to reformulate the question: 'are there nearly as many vacua as we commonly say there are?'—with the implication that we are perfectly well aware that we don't really think what, if our words are taken quite literally, we often say. If 'knowledge' were analogous to 'vacuum' the debate about scepti- cism would be very different; most likely it wouldn't exist at all— people would quickly take the sceptic's point, and pass on. Not only can one not see how an absolute concept of knowledge could have arisen; there is positive reason to think that it hasn't.

Unger saw this problem, or one very close to it. He observed[9] that when pressed to be accurate in our use of such terms as 'flat' we are inclined to say that we never did believe that (many of) the various surfaces which we called 'flat' really were flat, only that that they were flat enough for our then current purposes; but that in the case of 'know' we feel, even if we are convinced and finish up complete sceptics, that previously we really did believe that we knew (most of) the things we verbally claimed to know. But having pointed it out, Unger honestly admitted that he could give no explanation, and that to give one 'must remain a further question'. The answer, I believe, lies in giving up the thesis that 'know' is an absolute term, and then we shall have to take a more complex, and less partisan, view of the phenomenon of scepticism— which is what Unger himself later came to do.[10]

It seems then that there is no particular reason to continue with

[9] Ibid., (3), p. 89.
[10] It will be seen that my discussion of Unger throughout this section relates to his work up to 1976, when *Ignorance: A Case for Scepticism* was published. Since then his views have changed a good deal—see Appendix, below.

the unpromising search for practical factors that might decisively push objectivisation of the concept of knowledge to its theoretical limit—the indications are that it has not, at any rate not unequivocally, gone there. So we should pass to another highly pertinent question: are there any such factors that would cause objectivisation to stop at any definite and specifiable point?

We have seen the practical point of having a concept which requires that a belief be subjected to fairly stiff tests; the concept is applied only when the likelihood of its being false is very low. How low, or what possible ways of being false are to be considered, is variable. That the chief suspect might have an ulterior motive for confessing to the murder will often be taken very seriously; that the booking clerk might have an ulterior motive for telling me that the next train is due to leave in 5 minutes doesn't get a look in. (And this is not because false confessions to murder are frequent and must be allowed a fairly high probability, but because of what turns on the outcome.)

Only people who antecedently expect a concept to be loaded with all, strictly all, the conditions needed to determine its applicability to each instance, will suppose that we could in principle find, in the concept of the good informant (or of knowledge, for that matter), what distinguishes the Old Bailey from British Rail. Far more attractive is the supposition that the application of the concept is left to judgement, and that in human adults of a certain level of intelligence and experience judgement produces a workable degree of uniformity. It is a matter of taking appropriate care, and no mechanical directions for appropriateness are to be looked for in the concept itself.

Two thoughts occur. The one most immediately suggested by the foregoing is this: that the 'practically explicated' concept will simply be open-ended at this point. The concept of knowledge will make room for any, even the Cartesian, degree of caution in its application, provided there are purposes and circumstances to which that degree of caution is appropriate. The second thought pulls against this one, however. We have already agreed that the relevant level of caution will be fairly high—the practical requirement of objectivisation will put a fairly stringent lower bound on it. May there not be practical requirements that put some sort of upper bound on it as well? If so, do they perhaps shield the concept from confrontation with the possibilities traditionally used for generating scepticism? In that event, those who insist on confronting knowledge-claims with the

standard sceptical fantasies really would be straightforwardly misusing the concept—as has often been said of them.

Concentrating for the moment on the first of those questions,
we may say at once that there may well be some such requirements.
For a start, we have already observed that there are many 'possibilities', including the now standard sceptical scenarios, which are just
not treated as such in ordinary (meaning: non-philosophical) practice. Not that they are considered and jettisoned; they are simply
not considered, the very thought of them is something strange and
new to any adult who comes across them, which the great majority
never do. Now if standard practice thus excludes them, will they
not also be excluded from any role in determining the applicability
of the standard concept of which, presumably, standard practice
is constitutive?

Further, can it not be argued that this is more than just a descriptive
point about everyday practice? Such extreme possibilities are not
worth considering for the powerfully practical reason that their realisation would make no noticeable difference to us. Maybe virtually
all my beliefs would be false were the demon, or Berkeley's God,
in action. But then if the demon, or Berkeley's God, is in action,
acting on these beliefs will have, so far as I am concerned, just the
effect I wanted. There can be no practical advantage in trying to
distinguish between two situations which will be, so far as we can
tell, indistinguishable. And few enterprises are in this respect neutral;
where there is no advantage to be gained, there is nearly always
disadvantage in pursuing them. Had we unlimited time and energy,
then perhaps; but since we don't, their pursuit mostly distracts us
from what is more urgent. What we are looking at, after all, are
the factors giving rise to a very widespread feature of language—
certainly not an invention of the leisured classes.

There may be some truth in that thought when it is applied to
certain sceptical hypotheses, such as for instance that which postu-
lates a demon absolutely consistent in his deceptions now and hence-
forth. But the more disturbing hypotheses, practically speaking, are
ones that propose some sudden change, a demon whose powers
(or intentions) are wearing out, a deity bored with the present order,
or grown jealous of the enormous respect accorded to Fred as an
informant. Here we are threatened by practical consequences
enough, but still such possibilities play no real part in our thinking,
no matter how important it may be to us to acquire true beliefs.

For an explanation of this, however, we can look in another direction: no practical purpose can be served by a test which every informant is bound to fail. We do have to find someone who satisfies the test, for otherwise no informant, no belief, no action, no success. And no success, no survival. Let it be granted that there are compelling practical reasons for wishing to avoid falsehood, especially if it might fall at an important junction in our whole system of beliefs from which (like Descartes's rotten apple) it might infect many of the others. But if action needs belief, having false beliefs is no worse than not having any beliefs at all, so no practical motives could lead us to prefer the latter state to the former and impose tests that would expunge all belief before admitting a single falsehood. On the contrary, what that would indicate is the rejection of the tests. It looks as if the technique of practical explication will lead us to a concept immunised by its own limiting conditions against the sceptic's threat; and conversely, if the concept of knowledge is vulnerable to scepticism, no practical explication will be able to explain how it got that way.

This, however, must surely be the wrong way to argue. We have said that in everyday practice the idea of applying such tests as the standard sceptical fantasies just doesn't come into anyone's head. It follows that the opportunity to lay down the practice of rejecting this kind of test, either for the reason of its unsatisfiability or any other, equally just does not occur. We may conjecture about what would happen to an attempt to introduce such tests into everyday thinking—it isn't very hard—but that is not to say that everyday practice is already determinate on the point. It has after all neither need nor reason to be determinate. A decision isn't called for; no-one raises the question, no-one even entertains it, let alone seriously considers allowing such a test to affect the formation of his beliefs. Societies have laws; but no society has a law against doing something which it never enters anyone's head to do. (Though—and here lies the analogy—were someone to think of it and do it, there could well be a widespread, uncomfortable, and unenforceable feeling that somehow or other there had been a breach of something.)

We must not be mislead. There are, in a sense, factors which cause objectification to stop short of the sceptical fantasies: it is bound to stop short of considerations which are never considered. But that does not mean that the concept so formed acquires as it were a 'hard boundary' at this point. On the contrary, the operative fact is precisely that nothing happens here, so we neither have a positive boundary nor the positive absence of one. The resultant area of indeterminacy hosts the controversy about scepticism. On the one hand, the genesis of the concept through the process of objectivisation pushes us on towards acceptance of ever severer tests and so finally over the edge and into the arms of the sceptic; on the other, we are held back by the perception that the edge marks the end of any contact with the practical requirements which are the concept's ancestry. In much the same way, in a related area, the impetus of objectivisation pushes us towards the thought of a state of affairs which is in principle beyond our powers to recognise; and pragmatism causes us a bad conscience if we give way.

None of this fully explains the existence of scepticism. Nor ought it to, for scepticism is a philosophical phenomenon. Neither it, nor its rebuttal, forms any part of everyday practice, where the whole issue is simply unknown. And my style of explanation is suited only to explaining the state of everyday practice. What, drawing on the technique of practical explication, I have tried to make plainer, is the nature of the gap in the everyday concept in which the debate about scepticism can go on, should any philosopher find motive to start it up. The motive might be the prevalence of some metaphysic which suggested a particularly insightful grasp of reality. But it might equally be reflection on the everyday practice itself. For we do find there a tendency to seek to improve the reliability of our information, so that if the proponent of the sceptical argument says that he is merely inviting us to do a little more of what we normally do anyway, no decisive refutation of him will be available. He can extrapolate this tendency without doing anything which the concept of itself forbids; and such extrapolation will lead to scepticism. His opponents, on the other hand, can find in the normal rationale of everyday practice a reason for crying halt to the extrapolation before an irremediable scepticism sets in; their perception that some kind of non-arbitrary boundary has been crossed is no illusion. No more than the radical sceptic do they do anything which the ordinary concept of knowledge disallows. Quite the contrary, each of them does something which certain (and of course quite different) aspects of the concept encourage.

To try to go further and treat of the specific motivations which have lead some philosophers to exploit this situation would pass beyond the scope of this essay; it would mean introducing considerations which cannot possibly be thought to be part of the mental life of any and every human community. But since the notion of practice has been much to the fore in our argument, I shall end the section with a brief excursion designed to test the assumption that whatever the motives which might lead a philosopher to scepticism, they could not be ones having any practical bearings.

A plausible view, which I have already alluded to, is this: there are indeed very compelling practical motives for trying to avoid falsehood, especially if the falsehood might have the kind of centrality that could make it likely to infect many of our other beliefs. But survival calls for action, and action needs belief, so having false beliefs is no worse than not having any beliefs at all, and will often turn out a great deal better, hence no practical motives could lead us to prefer the latter state to the former and impose tests that would keep out falsehoods by rejecting everything.

On reflection, however, that argument can be seen to distort the order of investigation. If we are to be true to the notion of a practical motive we must not forget that practical motives have to operate in actual circumstances, and in actual circumstances we don't know in advance of applying a test what results it is going to give—or we would not be applying it. The Cartesian procedure opens with the thoroughly practical intention of avoiding falsehood. To make as certain as possible the attainment of this very practical aim it subjects beliefs to the strictest test it can devise. That is practically minded too: if we are going to do it let us have no half measures. If it now transpires (contrary to Descartes's own opinion, but in accordance with the views of many others then and since) that the test is too strict, and that hardly anything survives or proves reconstructable, that does nothing to show that the test was not in the first place practically motivated but at most that there can be no practical motivation for allowing it to dictate one's beliefs, and especially one's withholdings of belief, now that the outcome is known. Would the practically minded man have applied the test? Quite likely he would, unless prescient as well as practical.

But another aspect must not be forgotten. Perhaps he didn't need prescience after all. Perhaps something other than foreknowledge of the result of the test could have told him that there was something wrong with his enterprise, if conceived in the practical spirit of an attempt to eradicate falsehoods from the belief-corpus. Perhaps he could have seen that there were certain beliefs which he was not going to drop, no matter what the test told him about their status. If that is so, the position is different. It isn't exactly that there is no practical motivation for the test, but rather that the motivation is balanced by the inability to take advantage of it. There may be excellent reason for me to go to the shops—I need to buy something. But then there is the countervailing reason that I am too mean to buy anything when I get there. So I may just as well not go; and likewise if there are certain beliefs which I am not going to change, I may just as well not bother to investigate them.

The to-and-fro of the debate doesn't finish there, however. Other possibilities remain uninspected. For one, perhaps he couldn't have seen, without applying the test, that certain beliefs were going to stay with him no matter what its verdict. For another, perhaps in order to test those beliefs which he was capable of changing, he had to operate test procedures radical enough to induce doubt, or in some cases pseudo-doubt, in respect of all his beliefs, immovable ones included. For a third, even in the case of such 'immovable' beliefs, there may be practical benefits arising out of our attitude towards them and other beliefs consequential on them if they are subjected to a very rigorous test and are seen to pass it; in that event there could be a practical point in applying the test to them, even at the risk that they would fail it.

We are ill-equipped to deal with these thoughts, partly because we have too ill-defined a notion of what constitutes a practical benefit, and partly because (as in the second and third possibilities just mentioned) we are not clear enough about the boundary-conditions of the whole inquiry. But appeal to our ignorance, of which there is plenty in this area, will only serve to stave off an attempt to show that no practical motives could lead to the formation of a concept of knowledge capable of supporting, or in some way permitting, radical scepticism based on the argument from the thought of the demon. It cannot help with the positive task of showing how practical pressures could give rise to such a concept. That task is evidently beset by all manner of difficulty; there is no obstacle here to understanding the feeling that the argument from the possibility of the Cartesian demon invites us to abandon the very purpose of speaking of knowledge.

Two ideas about the way in which philosophical scepticism arises enjoy at present considerable currency. One often hears of the 'first-person' approach to epistemology; its *locus classicus* is held to be Descartes's first *Meditation*: the adoption of the stance of unaccompanied epistemological soloist is followed by catastrophic sceptical collapse. True, with one bound our hero is free, but that part of the story fools nobody nowadays, and didn't fool everybody at the time. The first of the two ideas, then, is that the stance is what causes the collapse. The second, associated in particular with Bernard Williams and Thomas Nagel,[1] is that scepticism is the offspring of an 'absolute' conception of truth, which encourages the attempt to know reality as it 'really' is independently of the perspective, capacities or interests of any observer. It is the search for what Nagel more figuratively calls 'the view from nowhere' that makes sceptics of us. I shall argue, on the contrary, that neither of these ideas is sufficient to explain the pull towards scepticism, nor the repulsion from it. I do not say that they have no part to play, because I do not think that there is just one route by which scepticism is reached—nor indeed just one position of which 'scepticism' is the univocal name. What I do say is that they require, at least, supplementation of the kind I have suggested in Section XII: something or other must be offered to explain why the standard sceptical stories (about demons, brains in vats and so on) should be thought to have anything to do with the business of knowledge, and why their connection with it should at the same time be felt to be so questionable.

The first-person approach is sometimes characterised as that which takes as its central question 'What do I know?' rather than the impersonal 'What is known?'. But that characterisation doesn't by itself capture any important distinction. In answering the former question I might be prepared to make uncritical use of 'what is known', the contents of almanacs and encyclopedias; in answering the latter

[1] Esp. B. A. O. Williams, (2), ch. 1, and T. Nagel, ch. 5.

on the other hand I might start by taking 'what is known' to be the aggregate of everything of which some individual can rightly say 'I know it'—and then all would turn on what I took to be the proper way of tackling the first-personal inquiry. It is a particular way of tackling that inquiry, I believe, which philosophers have in mind when they speak of the first-person approach to epistemology. In deciding what I know (and how I know it) I am not to make use of any material except what I can myself stand as authority for; no other person is for me a source of legitimate belief unless I am in a position to certify him as such.

A fairly platitudinous observation is that this restriction is likely to shorten the answer to our question 'What do I know?' a good deal. But that has little to do with scepticism. For scepticism to come into view we need the answer reduced to 'Very nearly nothing', or 'Nothing about the physical world', or something else of like brevity. If the first-person approach can do that it must have muscles we have not yet seen.

Here an aside: an argument has recently come into fashion, found by Kripke in Wittgenstein, which purports to show that an isolated individual cannot operate a language, but will be overtaken by what one might call semantic collapse. That would be quite catastrophic enough to count as a severely sceptical result, maybe the ultimate in scepticism. But whether it really follows, and on exactly which reading of 'isolated', are questions which mercifully need not detain us now; the history of the topic sufficiently instructs us that it isn't from arguments about rule-following that scepticism has emerged. The view that the isolated individual will never know anything because he will never get any concepts working, whatever its claim on us, is not what we are looking for at the moment.

Epistemologists are understandably afraid of the principle (which I shall continue to call the Iteration Principle as in Section VIII) that one only knows that p if one knows that one knows that p. They fear regress, both of beliefs and of reasons, which takes us far beyond what is actually the case and probably also beyond what possibly could be the case; down that hole lies radical scepticism. One may stop the regress by digging supposedly self-intimating foundations, but the only foundations with any claim to being self-intimating have turned out too flimsy to support much of a building—which brings us back to scepticism again. I agree, but I would point out that any connection between the acceptance of this principle and the adoption of the first-personal stance is very dubious, not to say wholly imaginary.

Does the first-person approach lead to the Iteration Principle and all concomitant difficulties? It could be thought to—and evidently has been, as we saw in Section VIII. If I ask 'Do I know whether p', and want to settle the matter myself, I will stop only when I have assured myself that my state (in most cases probably something about how I acquired the belief) is one which correlates well with being right on that sort of question. And that may look like saying that I will stop only when I reach the state of knowing that I know that p. Let us accept that; it surely does not amount to saying that I know that p entails that I know that I know that p. If it did, we would be faced with an absurdity. For consider the simpler case in which I, adopting the 'I'm going to settle it myself' posture, ask 'whether p?' Again, I will stop only when I have assured myself that p, and if I do it responsibly that will happen when I have got myself into a state that correlates very well with being right on that question, one which may fairly be called 'knowing that p'. But no-one will think (please!) on these or any other grounds that p entails 'I know that p'.

It may be said that I have to do a little more than that. If I responsibly investigate the question whether p then I must try to get myself into such a state and be convinced that I have succeeded, so that if, having carried out the investigation, I am asked whether I know that p, I will reply that I do. Let us agree; surely still nobody thinks on those grounds that p entails that I (or that they) know that p? The truth, altogether less barbed, is that anyone who has carried out a successful investigation will then know that p (or not-p, as the case may be); and anyone who thinks that they have carried out such an investigation will (understandably) think that they know that p. Hence—not as any consequence of the concept of knowledge but merely as a special case of the above—anyone who has carried out a successful investigation into whether or not they know that p will then (assuming that they do know it) know that they know that p. But nothing about this suggests for a moment that one cannot know that p without knowing that one knows. The Iteration Principle says that if one knows that p one knows that one knows that p, which is exciting and dangerous, but unfounded. What we have just reached says that if one knows that p and has successfully investigated the question whether one knows that p, then one knows that one knows that p; and this is very well founded, and completely harmless, and really quite boring. Its content is no more than this: that successful investigations result in knowledge.

There may however be a line from the first-person stance to scepticism which does not pass through the Iteration Principle. Perhaps it is not quite the form of scepticism we have had in mind in the paragraphs immediately preceding, but it is still quite sceptical enough to deserve the name. If we have adopted the first-person restriction and are interested in whether we know that p then it will not satisfy us just to know that p so long as the fact that we know that p remains opaque to us. Suppose that someone is in a position to assure me—quite likely it will be on the basis of an externalist analysis of knowledge—that provided I do have hands (provided neither demon nor computer-aided scientist is at work) I know that I have hands. Now—he will typically continue—you believe, indeed you have no shadow of doubt, that you do have hands, so without casting any greater shadow of doubt you may proceed to believe that you know it. I am offered a conditional with the observation that I am incapable of doubting the antecedent; and if I accept the conditional I had surely better abandon hope of ever showing that I don't know that I have hands, since for that I would have to show that I don't actually have any. But something seems to have gone missing, for I knew when I began that I had all these beliefs and could raise no real doubt about them; but I was worried by the thought that I could be in that state and the beliefs be false, for instance if I were subject to the demon, or were the consciousness of a brain in a vat. I wanted to get behind the fact that I have these beliefs and cannot doubt them, to see whether I could find a guarantee of their solidity which indubitability alone cannot provide, not, Moore-like, to re-affirm the beliefs and then, via an externalist analysis of knowledge, to conclude that they were known to be true as well as true *simpliciter*. And in that I failed: faced with the hypothesis of the demon and its like, I found myself just emptily repeating my own convictions without being able to point to anything on which they were based which would not equally be present were they false and any of the traditional sceptical hypotheses true. Isn't this scepticism? And doesn't it emerge from the first-person stance?

I shall not spend time on the first of those questions. To the second I would say 'No'. No, because the first-person stance by itself does nothing to explain why the fact that I can give no distinguishing marks by which to rule out *that* sort of possibility should have any significance for me at all. And once we allow that sort of possibility a place in our thoughts we will get the same effect whether we operate from the first-person stance or not. It can easily come to look otherwise, for if we ask 'Does Fred know that *p*?', why should we not use our knowledge that *p* as a baseline and start off by observing that *p* is true? None at all (that we have seen so far), unless we are going to allow the sceptical hypotheses their traditional role. Once we do that we shall find ourselves stuck on the thought that our decision that Fred does or does not know that *p* rests on our decision about *p*, which in turn rests on a belief which we hold in spite of the fact that, in the sceptic's story, it would be false although to us the world was indistinguishable from the world we are actually in—as we at any rate immovably believe.

Another point arises here. Once we have decided to admit the requirement that we be able to distinguish the circumstances involving the demon from those which, as we believe, actually obtain, we do not then need the first-person approach as an extra: we get it thrown in. For if we see the challenge in those terms there will be no point in responding by asking about someone else's knowledge, let alone trying to take someone else's opinion as ground-level evidence: even that there is anyone else will be a belief we can only be entitled to make use of once the challenge has been met. That Descartes first introduced himself in isolation and then thought of the demon is from this point of view an expository accident; he could just as well have thought of the demon and then have realised that this was one he was going to have to cope with on his own.

How may we summarise? It isn't (obviously) that first-personalism in epistemology doesn't exist, nor that it has nothing to do with scepticism. The point is that both first-personalism and scepticism result from thinking about certain possibilities (fully comprehensive dreams, demons, brains in vats, in general any hypothesis on which our cognitive faculties would give a systematically distorted view of large tracts of reality) which are normally ignored. If we want to understand scepticism we need to understand how and why such possibilities come to be taken seriously.

The other suggestion I want to discuss in this section is the idea that scepticism might be the outcome of the attempt to achieve an 'absolutist' view of truth. Bernard Williams writes of the 'absolute conception of reality', which he sees as a possible (concealed) source of Descartes's scepticism; Thomas Nagel writes of the attempt to reach an objective view, the 'view from nowhere', which shall have left behind all beliefs that are due to our particular character and situation. I begin by examining Nagel's position as found in chapter V of his book of that title. Here is a suitable quotation to start from:

Objectivity and scepticism are closely related: both develop from the idea that there is a real world in which we are contained, and that appearances result from our interaction with the rest of it. We cannot accept those appearances uncritically, but must try to understand what our own constitution contributes to them. To do this we try to develop an idea of the world with ourselves in it, an account of both ourselves and the world that includes an explanation of why it initially appears to us as it does. But this idea, since it is we who develop it, is likewise the product of interaction between us and the world, though the interaction is more complicated and more self-conscious than the original one. If the initial appearances cannot be relied upon because they depend on our constitution in ways that we do not fully understand, this more complex idea should be open to the same doubts, for whatever we use to understand certain interactions between ourselves and the world is not itself the object of that understanding. However often we may try to step outside of ourselves, something will have to stay behind the lens, something in us will determine the resulting picture, and this will give grounds for doubt that we are really getting any closer to reality.[2]

There seem to be two ideas playing leading roles here. One is—to let Nagel's metaphor go on running for a bit—that Nowhere is not a place on our map. In other words, whatever intellectual twists and turns we make, the result has still been reached by us, with our properties of mind and body. There is no way of reaching a belief without some of these playing a part in the process. The other idea is that of a theoretical advance which gives us good reason to believe, in particular cases, that certain apparent properties of reality are in fact contributions of ours, and should therefore have no place in our new view of what the world is objectively like. (A classic case, to which Nagel later refers, is that of secondary qualities: we form a conception of the world and our perception of it which explains why we perceive things as coloured without saying that they really are coloured.) The second of these, so Nagel

[2] Ibid., pp. 67–8.

implies in the quoted paragraph, leads us to the first, and the first (this seems to be said in the final sentence) gives us grounds for scepticism. We can't reach Nowhere, so the possibility of being wrong is ineradicable.

We need to be clear just how the train of thought is supposed to run. Why, for instance, should we be so keen on that last sentence (of my last paragraph)? Our beliefs are formed by us—that seems to be the literal content of the metaphor about Nowhere. Now if that thought, unaided by hidden premises, has sceptical consequences, then any belief-forming being must be subject to scepticism. The idea that God stands above scepticism, which afflicts only creatures, will have to be dropped, and the doctrine of his infallibility declared incoherent. One can avoid this conclusion only by identifying the facts with God's beliefs—so no wonder that something of the kind appears to have tempted some theologians. The hidden premise, that the belief that p is distinct from the fact that p, is the further, minimally realistic, premise which we are to add to 'Our beliefs are formed by us'. Nagel, it appears, is happy to add the slightly stronger premise that we form these beliefs in interaction with the facts, but that strengthening can hardly be the decisive factor in the production of scepticism—what if we formed them without interaction with the facts?

That premise is also part of the argument from the objectifying theoretical advance. We are to envisage a sequence of events, thus:

(1) The World (W) appears to me to be F—and I accordingly believe it to be F.

(2) I form a theory (T) about W—including me—which explains (amongst many other things) how W comes to appear F to me.

(3) According to T, W is not F.

(4) I come to believe T—on account of its great explanatory power—and give up my belief that W is F. (Whether or not it continues to appear to me to be F.)

Now it is at this stage that Nagel arrives (see the passage quoted above) at the thought: 'But this idea [I take it, the corpus of beliefs that constitute believing T], since it is we who develop it ...' He goes on: 'If the initial appearances cannot be relied upon because they depend upon our constitution in ways that we do not fully understand, this more complex idea should be open to the same

doubts . . .' But that is not obvious; at least, it is not obviously
a legitimate conclusion to draw from the fact that we have just experienced the sequence (1)–(4). For nothing rules out the possibility
that we shall, going on in pursuit of our fully objective view, arrive
at a theory T_n, likewise about W (and ourselves within W), which
explains everything that happens in W, including everything that
happens in us. And 'everything that happens in W' includes of course
the full story of how we started off with (1)—and suchlike appearances—and ended up with T_n. It goes without saying that it is we
—with all the properties that T_n attributes to us, and indeed by
virtue of some of them—who have arrived where we have arrived.
And it is we who are now reviewing that fact—but then our theory
explains how we can do so. And this theory, let us then suppose,
shows every sign of withstanding all subsequent discovery and experiment.

No doubt all this is wildly fanciful. But I cannot see that any
contemplation of the route from (1) to (4) can show it to be impossible. And just suppose it were to happen, what would then remain
of Nagel's metaphor that 'something will have to stay behind the
lens'? In so far as we have good reason (which *ex hypothesi* we
have) to believe T_n, we have good reason to believe that we have
finally grasped everything about ourselves, as well as what everything else is like independently of us.

Scepticism shouldn't arise from the thought that this complete
and wholly objective theory could never be formed. Perhaps it could,
for all we have seen. It may arise from a thought quite different
from the problem of completing the investigation of which (1)–(4)
represents one stage. Perhaps the whole of this enterprise, however
successful it may at some future time appear to have been, is dogged
by an invisible dog. Though invisible, the dog is nevertheless very
familiar: one of the traditional sceptical possibilities. Maybe the best
supported, most complete theory we could even imagine getting
would still be radically misleading; maybe there is some hitch in
our processes of belief-acquisition for which we could never have
any evidence.

If this is what we are left with, things are rather different. If scepticism depends on a concern for that kind of possibility, we still lack
an answer to the question why anyone should ever have been concerned about it. It is not clear, for all Nagel's exertions, that it
emerges as an inevitable by-product of the drive towards the objec-

tive view, if that is to be understood as the advance illustrated by our sequence (1)–(4). It may nevertheless have something to do with objectivity, when that is characterised slightly differently, and that is what I have in effect suggested.[3]

The business of the objectivisation of a concept might in a (very limited) sense be thought of as involving the formation of an objective theory of the world. To have even a minimally objectivised concept I must come to think of the world as containing other perspectives than the one that I have here and now. For one thing, it involves the recognition that there are other people, and that they may make (and with luck also pass on) judgements about objects which are available to me, constituents of my world; further, that these may be judgements which I, from my position and circumstances, am at present not able to make. If I am to benefit fully from their powers of judgement, I shall need a little more sophistication still: their judgements cannot always be taken over by me exactly as they made them, but need to be adjusted to take account of certain differences between their situation and mine. (Indexicals provide the commonest example: we must learn to judge their reference with an eye to the spatio-temporal location of the speaker.) In acquiring these capacities we are building a theory (at this stage a very elementary one) about a common world and the way in which different views of it lead to different judgements about it. This, it seems, is the same process as the one that Williams and Nagel are interested in, though possibly an earlier phase of it.[4]

One may think of these varying perspectives purely cognitively, as different vantage points from which different individuals or groups survey the facts. But we should also think of them teleologically: the different vantage points may, and frequently will, be associated with different capacities and purposes. It is this idea, I believe, that we need to engage if we are to get a view of those aspects of objectivisation that may point in the direction of scepticism.

Williams imagines two subjects, A and B, each claiming knowledge of aspects of the world, but representing it differently—perhaps because of something so simple as a difference of position, perhaps for more complex reasons like a difference of perceptual equipment or conceptual resources. If we accept their claims as claims to know-

---

[3] Principally in Section XII.
[4] Possibly an earlier phase than concerns Nagel; Williams—(2), p. 64—appears to have this kind of thing in mind when he writes of a 'very primitive example'.

ledge, he goes on, we need to 'form a conception of the world which *contains* A and B and their representations'. This is the same starting as that of Nagel that we examined earlier (although he expressed his problem in terms of our point of view, Williams more impersonally): we are to aim at a theory of reality which will explain why it seems to be F from a particular standpoint. And his finishing point is the same as well. Any picture we may come up with

... is open to the reflection, once more, that that is only one particular representation of it, our own, and that we have no independent point of leverage for raising this into the absolute representation of reality.[5]

No more than Nagel's (to all intents identical) argument does this lead to radical scepticism. What it describes is a particularly sophisticated version of the familiar process of correcting our own mistakes. It might sharpen our consciousness of the claims of fallibilism, and make us more alive to just how many of our present beliefs might have to go by the board before cognitive stability is reached. But that it can be reached, and that our investigative practices are leading us in the right direction even if the road may be longer and more disturbing than we thought, this need not be brought into question. Just why *any* view should be open to the reflection that it is 'only one particular representation' still stands to be explained. It is not explained by the undoubted fact that some views invite that reflection.

The idea that is here broached—that of the attempt to get a view of the world which will enable one to take account of the perspectives of others—does however have something to do with the debate about scepticism, and does have something to do with an important source of encouragement for the sceptic. In this Nagel and Williams are, I believe, right. But what does the trick is the way in which this procedure of objectivisation, as I have called it, acts to form the concept of knowledge; whereas they see it as it were pushing our conception of the world out of reach, always one step beyond the latest advance of our inquiry. What does not emerge (and cannot emerge from that style of argument) is why they think it impossible in principle for us ever to catch it up.

[5] Williams (2), p. 65.

XIV

It has long been a complaint that some of our colleagues, especially Great Dead Colleagues, tend to treat epistemology as if human beings were spectators of reality rather than active constituents of it. Such complaints have not often been very sharply focused, and terminological oppositions like that of the standpoint of the Cartesian consciousness versus Being-in-the-World have done little to help. We are now in a position to offer a small truth from the area towards which these high phrases foggily gesture. It is a modest truth, and hardly justifies the woolly charge against the Great Dead Colleagues, but at least it is true, and can be made tolerably perspicuous. Assuming agreement that the concept of knowledge calls for truth of belief across a range of circumstances, some of which at least must be non-factual, we can say that it bears, in this feature, a mark of its origins in the needs of an active being. The right sense of 'active' needs some care, however.

Why we should want to believe truths is a question we will come back to—for the moment let us start from the fact that we do. The decisive point is that we have a degree of choice as to what, and whom, we believe, and can therefore adopt strategies intended to improve our chances of coming to believe truths. Since these strategies are to operate, as we have seen, under conditions of partial ignorance, they need to be such as will work in a variety of conditions, not all of which can turn out to be realised. Suppose however that our beliefs were simply triggered in us by the environment, and further that there was no question of our intentionally selecting those circumstances most likely to trigger a true belief on a given question. Then there would be nothing left for us to do but simply to hope that the environment would treat us well and deal us true beliefs where we needed them.

Under such conditions a concept with counterfactual implications would be redundant. It is true that a partially ignorant being cannot pointfully try to produce an effect without adopting a counterfactually effective strategy; but one can perfectly well hope for an effect without being in the slightest bit concerned whether or not it would have occurred had circumstances been in any way different. Indeed, hoping that it would occur under circumstances differing from the actual sounds like another—and rather strange—enterprise, perhaps: hoping that its occurrence is probable. What the point of doing that might be, as distinct from hoping that it would occur, isn't at all clear: what might impel us to entertain a hope which would be satisfied if the event proved to have been likely, even if it didn't actually happen? I don't say that there could never, in any particular instance, be an answer to that question—sometimes one might be less concerned to be right than to avoid looking foolish. But that is not an answer so natural and comprehensive as to make us expect the counterfactual component of the concept to be as it is even if no active truth-seeking strategies were involved.

Notice that this argument does not call upon the fact that, generally speaking, we want our beliefs for certain purposes, to enable us to act successfully in certain ways. No doubt that is so, no doubt it has some significance for the theory of knowledge, and a great deal for the sociology of knowledge. But all that the present argument makes use of is the fact that we are active, mentally and otherwise, in seeking true beliefs; and it would hold even for a being whose interest in true beliefs, once acquired, was purely theoretical.

That brings us back to asking: why should we be interested in believing truths? This wider question has a clear place here, and a fundamental one. Counterfactuality may be a central feature of the concept of knowledge, but we arrived at it only as an inevitable feature of any well conducted search for truth. So why are we searching?

Imagine someone who watches certain events without the slightest need or wish to intervene in them—they do not affect him in any way that would cause him to prefer that the series should be just as it is rather than otherwise, or vice-versa. His natural equipment, let us suppose, causes him to form beliefs about what is happening. Since, *ex hypothesi*, it is a matter of complete indifference to him which events occur, and we have so far provided him with no other evaluatory principles, there is as yet no reason in sight why he should prefer these beliefs to be true rather than false, or indeed why he should be pleased (or sorry) that he has beliefs at all. What do we have to add to this neutral state for it to begin to make some difference to him whether his beliefs about what happens are true or not?

For a start, let us simply suppose that he prefers some events to others. If he is right in believing that A is about to occur, and he likes A, then something nice is coming up, if he is wrong then it isn't—and that makes a difference to him. But so long as we take it that he cannot actually affect what is going to happen, and don't feebly abandon our inquiry by assuming that he values being right *per se*, this still doesn't throw any light on why he should want his beliefs to be true. If A happens, then something nice happens, but whether he antecedently predicted A does not, in this very simple model, make A any nicer, or the non-occurrence of A any nastier. As soon as we get pleasures of anticipation and pains of disappointment into the model, the situation will of course change in this respect, so this one might call the first grade of cognitive involvement.

Given this grade of involvement, it does become the case that if he can exercise any sort of control over what he believes, he can affect something which it is in his interest to affect. Now he has a motive for selecting, if he can, between different ways of acquiring beliefs, but it is not yet by any means clear that he will choose to select beliefs for their likelihood of truth. Having a true belief that something nasty is inevitably on the way may well make life a good deal nastier than the nasty thing will in due course make it anyway; for that matter, having a false belief that something nasty is coming will be no better, up to the moment when it is falsified. He may decide that the pains of anticipation of the nasty are worse than those of disappointment at the non-eventuation of the nice, and opt so far as he can to believe in a thoroughly rosy future irrespective of its likelihood; or he may find it so enjoyable when things turn out better than expected that he aims at a deeply pessimistic set of beliefs in the hope of thus maximising the number of pleasant surprises; or he might prefer to avoid believing anything as far as possible. To explain the preference for truth from this standpoint we would therefore need a supplementary, and I would have thought far from compelling, hypothesis about the balance between these various (and presumably variable) psychological forces.

A second grade of involvement comes if we suppose that he can in some cases affect what happens. Then at last it does appear that he must come to value true beliefs. For he needs true beliefs about what will happen if he undertakes such and such a course of action, as well as about what will happen if he does nothing, but just lets things slide. Once this stage is reached he must develop an interest in training himself to form his beliefs in ways which reliably lead to truths. And if we also, as for any hint of realism we must, suppose him to be partially ignorant of the conditions under which he is operating, reliability must include the counterfactual property that the methods would still have produced true beliefs had the world been somewhat different.

Truth, and the counterfactual effectiveness of the processes used to reach it, are two of the principal features of both the concept of knowledge and that of a good informant. Active involvement enters twice, on my account: we want true beliefs because we are agents; and we actively seek the truth, which is why we must try to 'track' it, not merely hope to hit it. I cannot decisively rule out the possibility that these two features may be convincingly explained without calling on the fact that the concept of knowledge is a concept formed and operated by active beings who need to direct their activity. And I grant—at least I can find no argument to the contrary—that a pure spectator could in theory operate it. But why should he? To ignore the question is to accept that there is a practice, common to the vast majority of human beings, which mysteriously exists without any basis in the human situation. Answering it, on the other hand, won't be easy—for anyone who thinks that epistemology deals with a purely spectatorial side of our nature.

Certain writers have recently drawn attention to a principle about the transmission of knowledge, namely: that if someone who knows that p tells me that p, I myself then know that p. It codifies a widespread intuition, or perhaps I should say a widely accepted linguistic practice, according to which it is perfectly normal to speak of someone as knowing something just because he was told it by someone else who knew it. I don't acquire much, if any, understanding of the facts just by being told them; but I do, according to this practice, at least come to know what they are.

Now the obvious first impression is that the approach via the good informant will account for this feature of the concept of knowledge, for if a good informant on the question whether p tells me that p (or that not-p, as the case may be), do I not then myself become a good informant on that question? It seems so. For I am then as likely to be right as was whoever told me. If he was a good informant therefore, so now am I. And a second obvious point beckons: if he didn't know whether p then neither do I—unless I know it anyway, independently of his telling me. Likewise, if my informant was not likely to be right then neither am I—unless, again, for some independent reason I am likely to be right anyway. There certainly appears to be a promising symmetry here. In this section I shall investigate to what extent it will hold up under closer scrutiny. We shall find a good many lessons learnt earlier coming round again.

Let Fred be a good informant as to whether p. He has some property the possession of which makes it very likely that his opinion on that question will be true, and indeed it is true. Now suppose he tells Mabel. Is she now a good informant as to whether p?

If that is strictly all that happens, then of course she isn't. For her to be a good informant it must be the case that she will now tell us the truth, and that isn't yet guaranteed; Fred's assertion that p (suppose for convenience of exposition that that is the truth in question) may have had no effect on her whatsoever, and she may not otherwise have been disposed to tell us that p. Clearly we need to add something or other to the situation to make sure that she will have anything to say at all, let alone the truth. The absolute minimum we can add is that she is indeed disposed to tell us that p—which is the same as Fred told her.

That still leaves it open, however, for her disposition to have nothing to do with her interaction with Fred; perhaps she would have told us that anyway. In that event—so at least runs the natural reaction—whether or not she is a good informant as to whether p has nothing to do with his having told her that p, hence nothing to do with any questions about transmission. I am sure the reaction is right, but it may be worth a couple of paragraphs to follow it through.

To be judged a good informant, Mabel will need to be disposed to tell us the truth, and also to have an 'indicator-property'—one which correlates very well with being in possession of the truth on this kind of issue. The first we have just equipped her with: we stipulated that p is true, and that she is disposed to tell us that p. Does she have the second? Or rather, since she might have the second in some other way (perhaps she saw that the cat was on the mat before Fred told her it was): does she have the second by virtue of having been told that p by Fred? The answer to that, at this stage, is clearly that she does not; all we have yet posited is that what she will tell us is in fact the same as what Fred told her —nothing so far about any connection between the one event and the other. But before we go further there is one point we ought to know how to cope with. At least it is true of Mabel that what she will tell us is the same as what she was told by a person who was telling her the truth and was very likely to do so. Now that property is surely one which correlates excellently with her now telling us the truth; and in that case is it not a perfectly good indicator-property, and one which she possesses?

In a sense it is, but the sense is completely insubstantial. From the point of view of someone who may now use Mabel as an informant, let us say ourselves, it has no content. For since we do not think that Mabel's opinion depends on Fred's, we are in no position to judge that it is the same as Fred's unless we know independently what Fred's opinion was. And since we shall in any case have to believe that whatever Fred held on the subject whether p is very likely to have been true, it is then really Fred whom we shall be using as our informant on this question and not Mabel at all. Earlier, in Section III, we considered the case of someone who holds a true belief that p but is useless as an informant because we can only tell that his belief is true if we already know that p ourselves. What we have here is the same thing, but just as it were one link further down the chain of communication. What is needed is something or other about Mabel which enables us to judge what it was that Fred told her from what she tells us, something which we can detect in her without first knowing what Fred said; that is to say: at the very least some kind of reaction to Fred's assertion. Perhaps we have here the beginnings of the intuition that if Fred's knowledge is to be transmitted to Mabel, so that she too now knows that p, some kind of 'uptake' on her part is required.

What kind? We have implied that it will have to be at least enough for her to be disposed, *as a result* of being told that p by Fred, to tell us that p rather than that not-p, or nothing at all. Shouldn't we consider the freakish case in which we know that Mabel systematically distorts this kind of information, and so can gather from what she says that p is true although she actually tells us something else? But we have considered this sort of thing before, and we should make the same response now that we made in Section V. Such examples may at best succeed in showing that a certain condition is not strictly necessary, a point which, though worth noticing, shouldn't affect our conception of the prototypical case. But does this one even do that? If we have to work our way back to the proposition that p from Mabel's assertion that q it is at best doubtful whether she really is functioning as an informant as opposed to a source of information, and hence whether there is any real informant in this story apart from Fred. We can therefore confirm the implication: Mabel must react to Fred by acquiring the disposition to tell others what he told her.

To get a little nearer completeness, we may also spend a moment on the case in which the disposition acquired is simply to repeat Fred's words on request, maybe uncomprehendingly, as one might parrot a message in an unknown tongue (a reaction even more minimal than what I just now called the absolute minimum). Here any hesitation one may have felt over the previous case is surely absent: the only informant in the piece is Fred, and Mabel is no more functioning as an informant than is a page of a book, or a strip of magnetic tape on which Fred's speech is recorded. She must, it seems, be disposed genuinely to *tell* us whether p, not just to mimic the sounds which Fred made in response to that question.

Must she also believe what he told her, and so offer it to us as a belief of her own? That seems to have been Michael Welbourne's intuition about the conditions for the transmission of *knowledge*:

'I told him who she was but he didn't believe me' is a correct and sensible report of the frustration of the speaker's act of commoning knowledge by the hearer's refusal to accept it.[1]

Again, we find ourselves somewhere we have been before. Whether a good informant must believe what he tells the inquirer, like the question whether a knower must believe what he knows, is something that needs to be judged in the light of Colin Radford's examples of the French Canadian and the hesitant librarian.[2] We find ourselves in the penumbra of the conceptual practice: virtually all cases in which Mabel tells us that p will be cases in which she believes that p and would not tell us unless she did believe it. In our attempt to understand the practice we have to give that fact all the weight it deserves—without ignoring the word 'virtually'. We can say, if we want to, that Mabel must believe what Fred told her, so long as that 'must' heralds not a logically necessary condition but a description of the prototypical case—otherwise we invite an expedition into the penumbra, where there is no reason to expect that anything decisive can be made to happen.

So, with that cautionary note loudly sounded, we can allow ourselves to say that Mabel must believe what Fred told her, because Fred told her. Is that enough for her to be a good informant on the matter in hand? To put it another way: is that much 'uptake' sufficient for the property of being a good informant to be transmitted? It would not—so at any rate intuits Welbourne, and my intuitions concur—be sufficient for the transmission of knowledge. For suppose she mistakenly took Fred to be attempting a double bluff, that is to say, trying to get her to believe the opposite of what he said by trying to get her to believe that he was lying, when he knew perfectly well that he was telling the truth. Then she would end up believing what he told her, and believing it because that was what he told her (for had he told her that not-p, then not-p is what she would have believed)—but would she know that p?

---

[1] M. Welbourne, p. 93.   [2] Section V, above, and C. Radford.

Many will surely feel that she wouldn't. Mabel is suffering from the notorious false lemma, for if she were brought to realise that Fred isn't double bluffing, what would she then believe? Would she believe that not-p, because she would then think that he was merely (single) bluffing? Or that p, because she would then think that he wasn't bluffing at all? Or maybe nothing, because she then wouldn't know what to think he was up to? So far as our story goes, it could be any of these. Lucky old Mabel then, to have got the answer right after all.

Consider now the parallel question as to whether Mabel is a good informant. We, who want a good informant and are hoping that Mabel will do the job, believe that she is telling us what Fred told her; further that Fred was potentially a good informant, and if sincere in what he said actually was one. Probably at this stage we rate her chances of being right very high, but then we hear that she thinks that Fred was double-bluffing, and that in fact he wasn't. How are we now to assess the likelihood that what she tells us is the truth? We have to assess the relative likelihoods of two possibilities: that he was only bluffing—in which case she will be wrong— and that he wasn't bluffing at all—in which case she will be right. And all we have to go on is that something or other made her think he was double bluffing. We are all at sea.

Suppose, however, that we are in a position to make some such estimate. Suppose we become virtually certain, and rightly, that Fred was being perfectly sincere. Now we know, since we can work out the effect of her view that he was double-bluffing, that Mabel is just as likely to be right as Fred was, which means very likely indeed. But now we are in the position of knowing much more about the situation than Mabel does, and it is very doubtful whether we are using her as an informant as to whether p. What we are doing, rather, is using her as an informant (or maybe as a source of information) to find out what it was that Fred told her. On that quite different question she is a good informant—though she didn't get the title by inheritance from Fred, but by using her own eyes and ears. And once we have that piece of information, we can do the rest, reliably. She could not; from what we know about her, her route is altogether too hazardous.

That, then, is why it is not enough for Mabel to believe what Fred tells her, not even if she believes it because it is what he told her. What we want, it now seems, is that Fred should have been

sincere, and that Mabel should believe him to have been sincere
and believe what he told her (i.e. that p) for that reason. This appears
to be what Welbourne calls 'believing Fred', and holds to be necessary for the transmission of knowledge. And as far as Mabel's contribution is concerned, he takes it to be sufficient: 'All that is required
of a listener who understands a knowledgeable teller if the knowledge
is to be successfully transmitted to him is that he believe the teller'.[3]
Necessary it may be, but I doubt whether it is sufficient (even supposing that Fred satisfies all required conditions on the teller), for
we can repeat the recipe used at the previous stage and insert another
'deviant' link: let Mabel's (true) belief that Fred was being sincere
(and was 'speaking from knowledge' etc.) be reached by some weird
route involving a whole lot of false beliefs on her part; so structure
the story, if you will, that only an amazing series of coincidences
prevented her from discovering their falsity and thereupon taking
Fred to be lying, or falling into complete confusion as to whether
he was lying or not. Then whether the exchange leaves her knowing
what Fred knows becomes as doubtful as ever.

Perhaps, however, it isn't Welbourne's intention to define 'believing the speaker'; perhaps he is offering it as an undefined intuitive
notion. But if that is to succeed, then on my diagnosis it would
have to be just an unrecognised attempt to exclude all deviance from
the route by which Mabel arrives at her belief, to ensure by covert
stipulation that she is not prey to any false lemma. It would be
preferable, because ultimately more illuminating, not to accept it
as primitive but rather to ask what was involved. Then we would
come to see what work it was really doing.

[3] M. Welbourne, p. 5.

We have concentrated on the form 'knows whether p', where p is some proposition. But it hardly needs to be said that there are other locutions using the verb 'know'; particularly common are 'knows how to A', where 'A' stands for some verb or verb-phrase, such as 'swim' or 'ride a bicycle', and that in which 'know' takes a direct object, 'knows X'. Very frequently 'X' here designates a person, though by no means always: there are people who know the law, and those who know their Ming—not to mention those who know London, Japanese, and their onions.

It would be nice if our account of 'know' in the propositional context could be coaxed into throwing some light on these locutions as well. Otherwise we shall be left with an apparent ambiguity, a term whose semantics have (at least) two unrelated explanations. Obviously there are many such terms, but it would be uncomfortable to have to number 'know' amongst them. Ambiguity, in the sense in which homonyms are ambiguous, doesn't feel to be the right explanation here. There is, of course, one contrary indication for the locutions 'know that (or whether) p' and 'know X': very many languages translate 'know' differently in the two cases—as regards Europe, at least, English is very much in the minority.[1] This is just what one normally finds in the case of homonyms: they tend to be language-specific, and their ambiguity not reproducible in translation. But a further look at some of the linguistic facts nullifies any such suggestion. For instance: the German *Erkenntnis*, clearly related to the verb *kennen* (which is of course the form taking the direct object), is quite happily used to include 'know that p' cases; and *Erkenntnistheorie* (the theory of knowledge) is very far from restricting itself to the direct object version of the phenomenon. Similarly, Polish has *wiedzieć* (which takes a that-clause) and *znać* (direct object) and derives its expression for the theory of knowledge in general from the latter: *teoria poznania*. Hungarian has *tudni*

---

[1] Perhaps a minority of one, so far as I have yet been able to discover.

(*hogy*) = know (that) and *ismerni* + direct object. Again, the word for the theory of knowledge derives from the second: *ismeretelmelet*. Nor is any restriction to the direct object form implied in the French equivalent *théórie de la connaissance*, although *connaître* is used with the direct object construction. The theory of banking, which is understood to some degree by both economists and aircraft designers, is quite a different business—two quite different businesses, in fact.

It should be added that when we go outside Europe the outlook begins to change: English no longer looks like the odd man out. In the handful of African and Asian languages on which I could find a good informant, all without exception turned out to share the English pattern: they commonly translate 'know (that)' and 'know (somebody)' by the same word. In view of this there is no question of shelving the issue, saying that it is altogether too parochial a linguistic fact to expect our style of pragmatic synthesis to account for it, rather as if one had asked State of Nature Theory in political philosophy to explain some idiosyncracy found in only half a dozen of the world's constitutions. On the contrary, it is something very widespread. The obvious exceptions ('obvious', that is, when judged from the western edge of Europe), as I have just said, are only dubiously such; to use them as a smoke-screen would be to duck a pressing issue.

There are, however, a couple of methodological points on which we ought to dwell a little, since they will be important for the subsequent section as well as this one. My type of explanation is best suited to explaining why a certain concept or linguistic practice exists, why languages need expressions to fit certain pragmatically created slots, so to speak. Now if we regularly find the same word filling two slots it is fair to conclude that the slots must be related, and to try to specify the relationship. But we must be clear: there is no commitment to the view that, if two slots are related, one will find the same expression in each. Be the difference only grammatical (here a 'that' clause, there a direct object for instance), no practical explication, however impressive an example of its kind, can yield the result that all languages must use the same word in both places. If native speakers can make the distinction, in any way at all, then they *could* use two words to mark it. It may be said that if the roles are conceptually very similar the verbal distinction will in due course evolve away. Perhaps, but this has the unsteady feel of a piece of armchair linguistics. That logically anomalous features of natural languages don't persist sounds like a guess, and a philosopher's guess to boot, and on top of that a philosopher who has forgotten how often other philosophers have used alleged logical anomalies in grammar as an explanation of conceptual illusion. The fact that 'know that' and 'know someone' is an instance of a widespread linguistic pattern obliges us to look for a connection; but finding one wouldn't commit us to the view that the pattern must be universally observed, and it shouldn't surprise or distress us to find exceptions. We shall find the same with 'know how to'.

A second point, at which I have already hinted, is this: it is positively undesirable that our method be used to explain linguistic phenomena specific to a few individual languages. It will help here to remind ourselves of our starting-point and motivation. The idea was that since 'know' expresses a concept which, give or take a few niceties of usage, is found in all languages, we accordingly wanted to explain how its central core arises out of very general conditions of life such as must affect any language-using community, perhaps any community at all. There is no such motivation for trying to capture in our explanation semantic nuances or facts of grammar found in only a few individual languages. On the contrary, there is a strong motive for not doing so: if we picked up anything specific to one language, that would imply that this language had somehow remained more faithful to the origins of the concept of knowledge than had others. The implication would smack of chauvinism (the language in question is almost certain to be one of the few well known to the investigator); and besides that it would raise the question why this language had stuck so closely to those origins when others had not. And since some of those others would be languages obviously related to the favoured language, and some might even be amongst its indisputable ancestors, the question would very likely be totally intractable. On all counts, therefore, better to steer away.

Nothing of this sort seems to apply, however, to the construction 'knows + direct object', which is clearly extremely widespread—so back to business. At first glance it might look as if the obligation to exhibit some kind of connection between knowing Fred and knowing that it is raining was the simplest of things to discharge. We are frequently in the position of wanting information, not on some particular point (whether p), but on some particular subject-matter. We need an informant who knows a lot about it, whatever it is—without, perhaps, wanting to specify at this stage exactly what questions we need him to answer. So a way of talking arises suitable to express this need: we are looking for someone who 'knows X', where X is the subject-matter in question. Someone who 'knows the law', then, is simply someone who can give us the right answer to a lot of legal questions; and someone who knows Fred is simply someone who can tell us a lot of truths about Fred. Easy!

We must not underestimate the force of that way of looking at the direct-object construction in general; it can actually take us quite a long way towards understanding its relationship to the propositional use. But there are certain particular cases that resist, and one of the most important is precisely that in which the direct object of 'know' designates a person. I might, calling on resources of musicological scholarship (real and imaginary) come to know more about Schubert than anyone else, maybe even more than he knew himself. But however much I knew I still wouldn't know Schubert—for us nowadays that takes time-travel, not scholarship. In looking for a good informant about Schubert I am not (fortunately) looking for someone who knew Schubert; and if I did perchance come across a Viennese bicentenarian who knew Schubert he might well not be as good an informant as some expert who didn't.

So it looks as if knowing Fred cannot immediately and easily be linked with having information about Fred. It is certainly not equivalent to knowing a lot about him. The tendency of the discussion might make one equate it rather to standing, or having stood, in a perceptual relationship to Fred himself, having experienced Fred's person, if one may so put it. And this would fit very badly with the original suggestion that the concept of knowledge is unitary and arises in all its grammatical forms from the needs of an inquirer looking for a suitable informant.

Nevertheless, on closer examination of its logic, 'knows Fred' may not be quite as recalcitrant as at first appears. To start with, let us remind ourselves that the 'knows X' locution does not always resist the model of the informant, as is shown by our example of knowing the law. Rather it is certain values of X, for instance names of people or places, that cause the trouble, and this may be taken to suggest that what we are after here is something connected with particular types of object—it might be that for particular types of object, pre-eminently persons, there are particular areas of information that we are especially interested in, and that possessing information in these areas is hardly ever found except in those who have frequently been sensorily acquainted with them. That would bridge the gap between 'knowing Fred' and having information (of this special category) about him, and it would bridge it in a way which allows us to assimilate another fact of usage: that knowing Fred comes in degrees. For we may know Fred very well, quite well, or hardly at all, so to account for the locution we need some quantity of which someone can have a lot, or a bit, or very little, and if knowing Fred does after all have to do with having information about him, then how much information one has will fit this bill very nicely. The most that our earlier arguments have shown, then, is that this range of information is not correctly specified if we just call it, with complete generality, 'information about Fred'.

Admittedly, there is an alternative way of accounting for these facts which is less favourable to our project. It says that for certain values of X 'knowing X' means being from time to time sensorily related to X, perceiving X, or perhaps more generally 'being in the company of X'. Thus for non-perceptual objects, or more generally non-locatable objects, such as the law, knowing them is indeed to be understood in terms of possessing information about them. But for some objects, especially persons, knowing them is primarily a matter of being together with them, and related to having information about them only because and in so far as that is the normal outcome of being in their company. And being in someone's company has the required property of being (roughly) quantifiable: one may spend a lot, not much, or hardly any time with Fred.

It is gratifying, however, to see that this account fails decisively. Knowing Fred, whatever it may be, is not something that rises and falls with the length of time the subject is together with, or experiencing, Fred. I may have spent hours with that fellow-commuter, yet scarcely know him at all. On the other hand there are people in whose proximity I haven't spent anything like so long and yet know (clearly because of the manner of the contact with them) quite well. The refutation of the 'acquaintance' theory doesn't prove that the informational approach must be correct, but when one thinks of the sort of example that refutes the former one cannot but incline to the view that the latter is a very strong candidate: surely the key lies in how much, and the kind of, information about Fred that the subject's contact with him has yielded?

The impression is reinforced when one remembers that lack of information about someone can certainly tell against a claim to know them. There is no one question about them failure to answer which is conclusive, but as evidence of ignorance builds up (I don't know what he does for a living, whether he has any brothers or sisters, where he lives, how he likes to spend his spare time, and so on) my claim to know Fred will be gradually whittled away. And, significantly, no amount of evidence of sensory confrontation with him, the ability for instance to give the most detailed description of what he looks like or the clothes he usually wears, will reinstate it. 'How peculiar', it will be said, 'to know that much about Fred's appearance when he hardly seems to know Fred at all'.

Perhaps our problem should therefore be this: supposing that the usage 'knows Fred' is at core to be understood on the same kind of informational model that we have proposed for 'knows that p', can we explain the feeling that some degree of acquaintance with or experience of Fred is a necessary condition for it, and that without it no quantity of information about Fred is sufficient?

The best chances for a solution must surely lie along the following lines: the nature of life in society makes certain items of information about people of particular interest to us. We want to know what Fred may be able to do for us, whether he will be willing to do it, how we may best approach him—just to mention a few of the more self-interested of our concerns. Many of these will be the sort of things that are not apparent to casual, or even careful, sensory inspection of the person in question. But there often are people (other than Fred himself) who are good informants on these matters, and virtually always they are people who have spent quite a lot of time in Fred's company. It is true that one can imagine a good informant who has not—as in our above example of the world's greatest expert on Schubert—but it is notable that our example was imaginary, and one can be sure that if real examples exist they are very rare indeed. There may be persons who have corresponded with each other long and intimately without ever having met; no doubt a small number of amateur radio 'hams' are in this position. And it is significant that if one of them were asked whether he knew the other or not he might well have difficulty deciding what to say. At least he would not be likely to give a quick and firm 'No' just because they had never actually come face to face.

There is, in other words, information about Fred which, with very few exceptions, only people who are literally 'acquainted' with him possess. In seeking a good informant on such topics we therefore take ourselves to be looking for someone who has spent a good deal of time with—meaning in much the same place as—Fred. Whether that condition is strictly necessary or not is a question that might be best avoided, but if we must ask it the right answer is probably 'not'—which shouldn't lead us to think that an adequate account of the concept would not mention it at all. The position is much like the one we saw earlier,[2] when asking whether it is a necessary condition of knowing that the knower believe what he knows, and what we are in danger of getting blocked by is too much respect for the old analytic format of logical necessity and sufficiency, with all else consigned to silence.

Apart from terms designating persons, the most common values of X for which 'knows X' raises the issue of sensory acquaintance are expressions referring to places—'knows London', and the like. They pose no fresh problems, and in one respect they are less complicated. It is rather easier to state, in general, what sort of information about London we shall normally be looking for: how to get from A to B, where certain sorts of facility are to be found. The point of principle is unaffected, namely that this sort of knowledge is virtually never found in anyone who has not spent a good deal of time in London. Once we have seen this we need no longer be too worried about the prospect of establishing close contact between knowing that p and knowing X, close enough to shed a good deal of light on the linguistic data.

But still there is cause to go a little further. A small observation may show that the idea of acquaintance, or perhaps it should be interaction with, a person, has found its way deeply enough into the concept of knowledge to have an effect on the outward grammar of the direct-object form. When we are thinking of knowing things about Fred, the demise of Fred does not affect the tense in which we cast the verb: there are people around now who know a lot about Schubert (died 1828). But were that Viennese bicentenarian still alive today he would not know Schubert, though it might be true that he *knew* him, and quite likely that he would know a lot about him. The same holds if we substitute the name of a town for that of a person. True, an example of a town that no longer

_____
[2] Section II, above.

exists may be somewhat harder to light on; but one that has changed a lot will do just as well.

Our deliberations so far come to this: whilst there is clearly a heavy informational component to 'knows X', the past-tense pheno-menon that we have just seen indicates another element, one which—unlike possession of information about X—ceases with the cessation of X. One thing you can no longer do to X when X has ceased to be is, obviously enough, perceive it. But there are many other barriers to perceptual contact. One of the most common is spatial separation, and we do not change 'I know' to 'I knew' just because an acquaintance is now far away—we do that only when we feel we have 'lost touch'.

As to what this might in essence amount to, I offer a conjecture which at least has some of the right properties. What 'knows Fred' suggests (in addition to information) is a capacity which might be broadly described as the capacity to interact with Fred, and to do so more smoothly and successfully than is generally the case when two more or less randomly selected persons come into contact with each other. (Note, now we are talking of capacities, that the capacity to recognise Fred isn't of much use here. I don't know Queen Eliza-beth II, but I would be pretty good at recognising her; probably some people who do know her would be no better.) Only in the rarest cases will such a capacity exist in the absence of quite a lot of information about Fred—so the two ideas intertwine.

Compare now two other examples of 'knows X': 'knows Lon-don', and 'knows German'. The former surely implies an ability to get about in London, to find places one wants, and so on. It also implies possession of a good deal of information about London, but this is not really a separate thing, since an adult human who can find his way about virtually always knows what he is up to, and so can present his capacity to himself and others in informational form, even if only rather crudely. To ask whether capacity or infor-mation is primary would probably be idle, and in so far as there are pointers one way or the other they are variable and context-dependent. In 'knows German' the emphasis is slightly different: it seems far more closely connected to knowing how to do something than to knowing whether something is the case, much more like an ability to act than a capacity to inform, though this may well be just because people are on the whole less skilled at articulating their linguistic than their geographical abilities. It is worth noting that there are languages which commonly use the word for 'can' rather than 'know' in this connection: 'er *kann* Deutsch' is thoroughly colloquial for 'he knows German', and Welsh has a very similar construction.

The form 'knows X' can therefore sometimes imply (or maybe even just straightforwardly affirm) capacities to act in certain ways. Given that, it cannot be wild to conjecture that this factor may be in play when X is the name of a person. Persons enter into our lives in rather a lot of ways, so that we could hardly be expected to say just what capacities are meant, as one quite easily can where X names a town, and trivially can where it names a language. But we already have some idea from remarks I made[3] when speaking of the sort of information which, in our practical dealings with a person, we might find especially valuable. If we want to enlist Fred's help a useful person to have on our side will be someone who knows Fred: he will get a chance to broach the matter, and know how to go about it, where we wouldn't. If we want to cheer Fred up (I don't wish to make it sound as if manipulation were all that interested us), whom would we prefer to send in: a friend or a stranger? Knowing someone, being acquainted with them and familiar to them, oils the wheels and has a million uses.

The line pursued in the earlier paragraphs of this section related 'knows Fred' to 'knows that p'. This one relates it to 'know how to'. We therefore need a view of the relationship between this locution, which at first sight appears to ascribe a capacity, and the evidently informational 'knows that p'. Otherwise this attempt to relate 'knows (direct object)' to both might be thought to split it incomprehensibly in two. Besides, quite apart from knowing Fred, enough languages have both 'knows that' and 'knows how to' for this to be a question in its own right. This section has contained hints, but now they must be made more explicit.

[3] Above, p. 145.

On the face of it, 'knows how to' is synonymously replaceable by 'can': to say that Fred knows how to swim differs only verbally from saying that Fred can swim. (Some readers will intuitively feel that 'synonymous' is too strong, that the difference is a little more than verbal; they are right, but to avoid speaking of too many things at once I must ask them to wait—until p.157.) And 'Fred can swim' tells us something about what Fred can do, not about his capacity as an informant. What then of our hypothesis?

We can of course ask someone how to do X, as well as whether p, and getting the right answer to the former type of question is often every bit as important to us as the latter. This might appear to show that the inquirer and his informant have just as good a place when it comes to the 'how to' construction as they did when we were thinking about 'knows whether' and 'knows that'. Earlier, whilst discussing knowing whether p, we took as an example a person wanting to know the way; and I trust that this was not felt to be inappropriate or strained, in spite of the fact that such an inquirer would usually put his question in the form 'Can you tell me how to get to the Town Hall?' Agreed, he will often receive an answer in the imperative mood: go on down here to the traffic lights etc. But an answer in the indicative (it's down there on the right) is just as normal, and the state he attains, if successful, can perfectly well be described as having information, knowing that the Town Hall lies in such and such a direction, or 'knowing where the Town Hall is'; and he could equally well have asked his question in those words ('Could you tell me where the Town Hall is?')—we often do. This isn't surprising. There are many things which, under anything like normal circumstances, we can do as soon as we have a certain piece of information—nothing but ignorance is in the way. Conversely, there are very many abilities which, except in freakish circumstances, people do not have unless they also have conscious access to a certain item of information. So for practical purposes the two locutions can then be treated as equivalents.

This is encouraging, but it shouldn't be taken to dispose of the problem. When we wonder whether that lady knows how to get to the Town Hall, then, it is true, we are nearly always wondering whether she will be able to give us information that will enable us to get there. But when we agonise over whether a child 'knows how to get home' we are worried about whether it can find its way home, not whether it can efficiently direct us there; clearly it might be able to do the former unfailingly whilst being hopelessly bad at the latter. What we are apparently concerned with here is a use of 'knows how to' which is at least nearly synonymous with 'can', and this seems prima facie to have no connection with competence as an informant.

As with the direct object construction, a simple claim of ambiguity is far too implausible an escape route. Besides, it would leave us wondering why so many other expressions, none of them with any feel of ambiguity, consort equally freely with both 'that *p*' and 'how to *A*': 'learn', 'teach', 'forget', and 'remember'. Furthermore, when the same ambiguity is found in a number of languages, especially if they are not all related, pressure builds up against the view that it is an ambiguity at all. So the claim would give a hostage to linguistic fact; and (to anticipate) linguistic fact is against it.

What responses are open to us? One might be to protest that we should not be expected to explain all features of usage; presumably many factors are at work shaping linguistic history. Now if we are thinking of features of usage specific to one or a few languages we should uphold the protest, as was argued in the preceding section. But if whatever is in question is found in almost every language the position is different. Failure to illuminate one such feature doesn't, strictly speaking, invalidate a putative explanation of another. But it would be feeble to hide behind that formal point, when the near universality of both features cries out for the same kind of treatment. And since these features concern the usage of the same word, there are obvious theoretical advantages in a unitary explanation which makes it understandable that the word should be the same in each construction. So this protest would really be just an admission of partial failure, a dive for cover; we should forget it.

There seem to be three strategies which may offer a satisfactory account of 'knows how to'. The trouble arose because that expression appears to have a sense in which it means that the subject can perform a certain kind of action. One way round the obstacle would be to disperse it by arguing that this capacity sense, although found, does not have the empirical status to be a problem: whilst it occurs in some languages, it is not so widely distributed as to be a proper subject of the present investigation. A second would be to argue that, first intuitions notwithstanding, the apparent capacity sense is really nothing of the kind, but informational after all. The third is to accept both existence and status of the capacity sense and then, by exhibiting a natural connection between the ideas of information and agency, explain how knowing that p and being able to A come to attract the same word.

How widespread is 'knows how to'? That is the crucial question for Strategy One. We are to focus on the obvious way, or ways, of rendering the English 'knows whether p' in a given language— 'obvious ways', to indicate that we are not to be sidetracked into subtle distinctions of nuance, references to the ways the words used in the respective language feature in specialised contexts, and so on. (We are not interested, for example, in whether the expression that corresponds to 'knows' in the Arabic for 'He knows whether it rained yesterday' is ever used in what is sometimes called the 'biblical' sense.) Having thus located the analogue(s) of 'know' in 'know whether', we consider the resources standardly available to a speaker of the given language for describing someone who, as we would say, can swim, and we look to see whether they (all or some of them) include the 'knows' component from the first group of expressions (or something closely related to it). If at least one of them does, then the given language has the capacity sense of 'know'.

Notice that the exact grammatical structure, knows how to + infinitive, is not our real topic. What we are really talking about are capacity-attributions which use 'know' or its obvious correspondents in other languages. It is that, and not any grammatical isomorphism, that we are to concentrate on.[1]

---

[1] The nearest German equivalent, for instance, is 'Er weiß wie man schwimmt'. But what this suggests most strongly is that the subject can tell us the theory of swimming, not that he can swim. Finnish (I am told) also has a construction verbally close to the English 'knows how to'; but again the import is theoretical. I understand that Hungarian, on the other hand, uses the word for 'know' with the infinitive as its standard colloquial way of saying 'can'.

So, does the capacity sense of 'know' have status or not? Here we need the empirical facts. We won't of course be able to get all the empirical facts; we shall have to be content with (or exhausted by) the facts about a few particularly prestigious (i.e. well-known) dead languages and a representative selection of living ones. Living languages are pretty numerous—a few thousand, on any sensible criterion for distinguishing them from each other—so we must hope to be representative without having to run our test on more than a small fraction of them. Our best bet will be to rely on the classifications of languages agreed among comparative linguists, and hope to find the resources (which is to say an obliging, educated, expert speaker) for testing a few members of each of the main groups.

These tests, so far as I have been able to carry them out, support the contention that the capacity-ascribing sense, if we can rely on our intuitive impressions to detect it, is at the least very widespread. Since the honest policy, and the only one that can lead to a genuinely robust theory, is to confront directly anything recalcitrant which looks as if it probably holds, it seems that we should accept that there is a prima facie capacity-related component of the concept, and try to explain the fact.

If anyone is determined not to accept it, they will be able to create a little room for manœuvre by playing on a methodological difficulty in the application of this test. I have already hinted at it: we cannot work solely with formal features of grammar, but must rely to a considerable extent on the semantic intuitions of native speakers. There may be languages[2] which have expressions that are close verbal parallels to the English 'know how to' without its being clear that they have the same meaning. Assume (for the moment) that the English 'knows how to' is a synonym of 'can'; it might be that in some languages there is a verbal equivalent of 'knows how to' which is semantically informational in content, that is to say: it is applied only to subjects who can tell us the way to perform whatever action is in question, or (a very different thing), the theory of its performance. In that case the mere existence of the verbal equivalent would not qualify that language for inclusion. Worse, there may be problems in determining the facts here; it may not be clear what sense, capacity or informational, a given expression has. We can experience the sort of difficulties that arise by consider-

---

[2] And so there are: n. 1 above.

ing the English expression itself, and we can kill two birds with one stone by doing it in the context of the second of the three possible strategies.

The second strategy is to deny that 'knows how to' has a capacity-sense after all. First appearances notwithstanding, we might argue, it indicates the possession of information about the performance of the action specified, perhaps even (we shall soon see that this is a little more) the capacity to give information about it. There are two broad types of position that such an argument might aim at. One would be the view that behind any exercise of ability lurks the deployment of information: if you can swim, that is always because you know that such and such is the way to swim, and can apply that knowledge. When, attributing to you the ability to swim, we say that you 'know how to swim', the word 'know' is being used with reference to the essential informational background, the 'knowing that'; and the change from 'that' to 'how' marks the fact that we are dealing with information of the type which character-istically enables a certain kind of action. This position is not far from the doctrine which Gilbert Ryle[3] called, and attacked as, 'intellectualism'—we shall shortly look to see whether his attack leaves any of it standing that might be of interest to us.

That short statement is enough to expose the difficulty I referred to in the previous paragraph. We wanted to be able to decide whether or not a given language uses its literal equivalent of 'knows how to' in a capacity-attributing sense. But, supposing for the moment the truth of the 'intellectualist' doctrine just outlined, how would we determine whether the word 'know' really referred to the state of information, or whether it was primarily a way of attributing the ability? If a capacity is always based on information, how shall we decide which of the two the expression 'knows how to' really describes? It looks as if we may have to accept a commitment to extensive quantities of semantic theory, something which the project was designed precisely to avoid.

The proper way to deal with this difficulty, I am convinced, is simply to bypass the argument and confront the least favourable alternative head on. Where two descriptions of the situation are possible, and a decision between them, if not arbitrary, would have to be grounded deep in the theory of meaning, we should treat

[3] See G. Ryle, ch. II, esp. pp. 30–2.

it either under both, or under the one likely to cause our hypothesis the most trouble. Thus, going back to our first strategy, we can see that it will cause the more difficulty the more languages are deemed to operate a capacity sense of their word for 'know'; so our principle recommends that we decide in favour of the capacity sense wherever there are not clear reasons to the contrary. In other words, we should acknowledge our obligations and commit ourselves to the third strategy. Otherwise we invite the charge of either ignoring the linguistic facts or trying to bury them under a pile of controversial semantic theory.

In any case, the train of thought we were considering is set in motion by an 'intellectualist' account of knowing how, and in view of that it may well be asked whether it is worth considering at all. Hasn't intellectualism been refuted? Ryle, one must admit, gave strong reason for thinking that, when taken in strict generality as applying to every capacity, it must be false: it leads to infinite regress. I accept the argument and its conclusion—a little casually perhaps, but that will do no harm in this context since it doesn't settle the present issue. For what Ryle showed was that some capacities must just be things which we can simply do when occasion arises. So intellectualism (i) can be true of at most nearly all our capacities, and (ii) cannot be supported by any general argument to the effect that capacity entails information. Good—but suppose that it were true of nearly all our capacities, and that that belief rested on common observation rather than any grasp of logical connection. That would be compatible with all that the argument from regress proves, but it would still be quite enough to explain how a concept which originated in the need for good informants should grow to encompass abilities as well.

But is it true, even in this weakened form? More exactly, does being able to tell us how to A go with being able to A, in our experience, in a sufficient proportion of cases for there to be any plausibility in the claim that the concept of knowledge spreads from the former to the latter precisely because of such concomitance? That must be very doubtful. Remember that when we speak of information we are speaking of being a good informant, not of information in the sense in which cognitive psychology might use the word. It is clear that the child who can unfailingly find the way home must in that sense have a great deal of stored information, and the same holds of anyone who can swim, ride a bicycle, or do anything else; but just as clearly, that is no guarantee of being able to produce it in a form that an inquirer can make use of, nor of oneself having access to the information in the form of conscious belief, nor even of having any practicable way of gaining such access. Having information, in this sense, has nothing to do with being a good informant, even potentially.

We must not, therefore, by conflating these senses of 'information', allow ourselves to exaggerate the degree to which capacity as agent goes along with capacity as informant. We should also beware of another factor which might lead us to exaggerate it. Any reasonably articulate person, if he can do something or other, will in many cases (not all) be able to tell us something of how it is done. But it may be that he does that by observing himself doing it, and then describing what he observes; in such cases the connection between having the ability and being a (more or less) good informant about how to do it is a wholly external one. If he saw someone else doing it he might then be just as good at telling us how it was done, in certain cases he might even be better. Now this type of case, though it does produce a certain degree of concomitance between having an ability and having information, we really ought to discount—it does little to explain why there should be a linguistic connection between being able to say how something is done, and being able to do it oneself. It is on a par with the fact that someone who has a dog is likely to be able to tell us at least a little about dogs; that hasn't generated a linguistic link between owning an X and knowing about Xs—nor would anyone expect it to have done so.

The hope of the second strategy was to find grounds for denying that 'knowing how' really has a capacity-ascribing sense. Our admittedly inconclusive discussion has by its very inconclusiveness pointed us towards the third strategy: that of accepting such a sense, and then arguing that knowing how to A lies, in so many cases, so close to being a good informant about A-ing as to make it perfectly comprehensible that a concept which has its seat in the idea of information should include the possession of capacities to act as well. But in pursuing Strategy Three we shall find a little hint of Two pushing its way in. 'Know how to' is indeed closely related to 'can', but not so closely as to justify the assertion of synonymy; and pragmatic reasons can be found to back up the common intuition mentioned at the beginning of this section, that 'knows how to' is at any rate not a pure ascription of capacity.

An underlying connection which can account for the overlap in usage is, in fact, not so hard to find. We may start with the obvious point that human beings need both true beliefs and capacities to act, since every action calls for both. The inquirer seeks a true belief on the question whether p; the apprentice, as we may call him, seeks the capacity to do A. His purposes may be furthered either by someone who tells him, or by someone who shows him, how to do A. So we may consider three cases:

(a) The inquirer, who wants someone to tell him whether p
(b) The apprentice, who wants either (i) someone to tell him how to do A, or (ii) someone to show him how to do A.

What we want, as apprentices, is to be able to do A ourselves. That being so, someone who can show us how to do it will be just as valuable as someone who tells us, so long as that has the same effect: that we can then do it. And of course people who can show us how to do it are invariably people who, at least to some degree, can do it themselves. We want to be able to do A, and in many cases we will be equally well served by an informant, who tells us that such-and-such is the way to do it, and an instructor, who shows us how to do it by doing it himself in front of us. And if we are equally well served by either, that will be a factor tending to encourage the use of the same term in both cases. When nothing much turns on the distinction there can be no surprise if we employ the same vocabulary; that is just what is suggested by the idea of a general term.

So the three cases begin to huddle together. There are obvious affinities between (a) and (b)(i), both of which involve the linguistic transfer of propositional information. And we have already observed that there are affinities between (b)(i) and (b)(ii): for a start, they are both widely used and effective means to the same end. On top of that, they are not always even distinguishable, for showing and telling may merge, and often do: 'Hold the two needles together, do you see, then take the wool, here, and pass it round one needle, so, and then take it between the needles like this . . .'

Other factors help to bind (b)(i) and (b)(ii). There is a class of cases in which telling and showing, knowing whether and knowing how, informing and demonstrating, merge; this time not as a contingent matter of normal practice, as in the knitting example, but as a matter of principle. These occur when doing the relevant A involves giving some verbal or at least symbolic performance, when to do A is to articulate some propositional information. Knowing how to prove Pythagoras' theorem is hardly distinguishable from knowing that it is proved like this: and there follows a sequence of propositional statements; telling and showing the pupil how to prove the theorem scarcely differ. It may be thought that such cases are rather too specialised to make a significant contribution to the shaping of usage. But that is very doubtful, since from one perspective a huge class of cases turns out to be of this kind. Suppose we think of the informant as doing something, namely answering the question 'whether p?', and doing it correctly. There isn't anything contorted about this: answering a question is really a fairly central case of an action, and perfectly naturally seen as such. There is an intended effect, a choice of means, the production of the effect by controlled bodily movements. One may choose the wrong end— affirm p when one should have denied it—and the wrong means— mispronounce the words, phrase one's answer clumsily or incomprehensibly. In the same way one can knock in a nail when one should have used a screw, knock the nail in badly—on a slant, or only half way—or miss it altogether. No-one need apologise for thinking of the informant as performing an action; on the contrary, the onus rests with anyone who denies it. So if Fred knows that p, if he is in possession of the information, he knows how to perform a certain action—how to answer the question whether p. Thus the link between possession of information and possession of a capacity is further strengthened.

We have seen[4] that there are languages in which the nearest verbal equivalent of the 'know how to A' construction carries a heavy suggestion that what is in question is theoretical, articulable, knowledge of 'how A-ing is done', which need not be accompanied by any ability actually to do it. And I think it is fair to say that there is a little—in some cases a very little—of this feeling about the English expression. We need to distinguish two points:

(1) That 'S knows how to do A' can be true when 'S can do A' would be false, for instance, if S has lost the requisite physical powers.
(2) That 'S knows how to do A' differs from 'S can do A' in

_____
[4] See p. 151, n. 1.

an implication that S has or can call up some degree of reflective grasp of the way to do A.

Both of these features are easily understood if we think of them in the light of the apprentice's situation. He wants to be able to do A, and is indifferent between (b)(i) and (b)(ii) as ways of bringing this about, or at least of bringing it nearer. Now it is generally true that someone who can satisfy his demands by the first method, who can say how to do it in sufficient detail and in such a way as significantly to help him towards being able to do it, will be someone who can do it himself. And anyone who can help him by the second method—that of demonstrating it—will obviously be someone who can himself do A. Hence the feeling that the apprentice must be looking for someone who can do A, and hence, on my hypothesis, the feeling that 'S knows how to do A' entails 'S can do A'. But since there are cases—the most frequent is probably that of the ageing expert who has lost the necessary physical powers—in which someone who cannot use (b)(ii) may still be a most effective operator of (b)(i), the apprentice's turn can be served by someone who cannot do A. Hence the existence of counter-examples to the thesis that 'knows how' entails 'can'. And this explains the existence of the feature (1). The situation is very much like that encountered when one asks whether 'S knows that p' entails 'S believes that p'. Believing is indeed central to knowing, but still one can find plausible counterexamples against the entailment claim. We saw that our method could explain that fact, and it can also explain the similar fact about the relationship between 'knows how to' and 'can'.

We can also explain feature (2). In the case of many activities, just performing them under the eye of the apprentice will not be very effective. Far more effective will be a self-conscious, reflective demonstration in which the teacher draws attention to the essential features of the performance, perhaps doing some of them more slowly, or exaggerating them slightly. To do that calls, obviously, for a little more on the teacher's part than the bare ability to do A; it calls for a degree of conscious understanding of the process. And that is just what feature (2) consists in.

It might be thought that this whole idea faces a tricky objection. Being a good informant, as we have seen, means more than just being right; in addition to that the good informant must possess some characteristic that makes him recognisable as such and supports confidence in his information. That was why the concept we constructed from the idea of the inquirer's search matched popular analyses of the concept of knowledge in calling for true belief plus satisfaction of some further condition. Now we are trying, by comparing the situation and needs of the apprentice to those of the inquirer, to assimilate 'knowing how' to being a good informant. So a person who knows how to do A ought in the first instance to be someone who (1) can do A, (2) is prepared to display A-ing, and (3) satisfies some further condition which advertises (to the sufficiently discerning) his fulfilment of (1) and (2); that would give us the desired parallel with the good informant, who can tell us the truth about p, is prepared to do so, and has some property which reliably indicates it. But not so, surely: knowing how to do A is just concerned with (1), being able to do A, and not at all with (2) and (3). The parallel collapses.

The objection is, I believe, confused. As regards condition (2), we should remember that there was the same problem over knowing whether p. A good informant should be prepared to assert that p, or that not-p, if that is his belief; whereas a knower (remember Luigi) may not be. There we had recourse to the idea of the growing objectivisation of a concept, and the same device will be available here; there is no asymmetry at this point. But still there may be asymmetry at (3). Doesn't the difficulty remain that knowing how to do A is concerned with (1), perhaps related to (2), but has nothing to do with (3)?

It is not straightforwardly true, however—as the objection implied—that knowing how to A has to do with (1) and not (3). That depends on how (1) is to be understood. There is after all a minimal conception of 'can', the one enshrined in the old logical dictum *ab esse ad posse valet consequentia*, in which I can do A if I bring it off, even though my doing so was a monstrous fluke which I am most unlikely ever to repeat. One who says that if you can do A then you know how to do A is certainly not thinking of this sense of 'can', but of something much more substantial: that there is something about you which makes you at least fairly reliable when it comes to A-ing. And what that means, it will at once be seen, is that if 'can' be taken substantially then the requirement (3) is already built in; whereas if it be taken minimally we need the explicit addition of (3) to reach anything recognisably like knowing how. The supposed asymmetry disappears.

It would in fact be both surprising and perplexing if there were any serious failure of parallel between knowing how and knowing whether. For if answering an inquirer's question is an action, and as such something that can be done successfully and unsuccessfully, in the right way and in the wrong way, then every case of knowing whether just is a certain type of knowing how; that is no less true just because it is a rather specialised case of it.

Possibly certain asymmetries do remain, though if so they are not such as to do any damage to our thesis; on the contrary, they are comfortably explicable in terms of it. Of the many types of action which one might wish to have done, or see demonstrated, the vast majority virtually never happen by accident. That means that a single performance given to order often has, *de facto*, the force of a proof that the performer can perform reliably. In contrast, there are many questions that can be answered correctly by accident, so that getting the answer right once only rarely establishes much likelihood that the informant will be right in future on that type of question. This point affects, however, not the parallel between the conditions for knowing how and those for knowing that, but only the ways in which we can establish that they are satisfied in a given case. A second asymmetry has just the same effect: someone who cannot himself do A may have no difficulty in recognising just by observing his performance that someone else is doing it; whereas someone who does not yet know whether *p* cannot tell just from hearing it affirmed that *p* (or not-*p*, as the case may be) that he has been told the truth. This means that whilst in the case of knowing *that* a great deal of strain falls on features of the informant which make it likely that his answer will be true, in the case of knowing *how* the corresponding facts about the agent seem of little import-ance. The cases in which we have to know that somebody is good at A-ing in order to know that A-ing is what he is now doing are by comparison rather rare. Mostly, therefore, if someone comes along and does A those who see it will at once, and very reasonably, take him to know how to do A. That does not mean that nothing more than his actually doing A is involved; but it may do something to explain the tendency to think that nothing more is involved, and to suppose—notice that this is in effect the point from which our objection began—that 'knows how' requires nothing more than 'can'.

We should not therefore be worried by these apparent disanalo-
gies. They only concern differences in the epistemology of the two
notions: how we tell whether a subject knows whether p, and knows
how to do A. Far more impressive is the close similarity of structure
between knowing how and knowing that, something which the dis-
analogies leave untouched. But we should remember that in these
last few pages we have only been countering an objection, not making
a part of our positive case. The fact that the two notions both involve
a success-clause plus a clause indicating that the success is no accident
is encouraging, but it does not of itself go far towards explaining
why the constructions by which they are expressed should use the
same word. For the positive reasons as to why this should happen
in so many languages we look back to the materials assembled in
the earlier paragraphs of this section.

APPENDIX: UNGER'S SEMANTIC RELATIVISM

A part of Section XII was directed to material that Unger published in 1976 in his book *Ignorance—a Case for Scepticism*. Since then there has appeared his *Philosophical Relativity* (1984) in which he expresses views incompatible with those of the earlier work. It would therefore seem only fair to ask how his new position relates to my remarks, both critical and positive; besides, what he says has great intrinsic interest, so that it is not just on grounds of fairness that it demands our attention.

In his second book Unger introduces an innovatory distinction between 'Invariantist' and 'Contextualist' semantics.[1] To be an invariantist with respect to the semantics of a particular term is to hold that there is a single standard for its correct use which applies in all contexts in which it is or may be employed. A contextualist, on the other hand, holds that the standard for its application changes with the context of utterance. Since each regards these standards as determining what the word means, this amounts to saying that it has one meaning (and one set of truth-conditions) for the invariantist, many (dependent upon context) for the contextualist.

Unger's next move is to argue that there is no way of settling the question whether the semantics of a given expression are invariant or context-dependent. The hard data of semantic theory are the utterances of speakers and the reactions of hearers, and these underdetermine the (supposedly) factual matter at issue between invariantist and contextualist. The difference between the two types of theory lies in where each locates the complexity which must undoubtedly characterise the process by which competent speakers pass from situation to appropriate utterance, and from utterance to appropriate reaction. The contextualist makes semantic understanding, the grasp of what has literally been said, highly complex: we have to work out just what that utterance means in that context. For the invariantist that stage is comparatively easy: we just have to grasp what

[1] See P. Unger, (4), pp. 6 ff.

the utterance means, a matter to which the context of utterance is irrelevant. But then, for the invariantist, comes the complexity: we have to be able to judge just how much, and what kind of, departure from the one invariant semantic standard is acceptable in the given context. Each theory has to balance the budget: one buys simplicity here for complexity there, the other pays complexity here for simplicity there. How much complexity has to be postulated may well be an empirically determinate issue, but where it falls, Unger argues, is not. Neither, therefore, is the debate between invariantist and contextualist, since this is the very point on which it turns.

Now Unger's previous argument to scepticism was based on the lemma that 'know' is an absolute term; and to regard something as an absolute term is to ascribe to it invariant semantics. (It was because he then took it that knowing calls for absolute certainty—than which nothing could be more certain—and calls for it invariantly, context-independently, every time it is uttered, that Unger could pass to the radically sceptical conclusion that virtually every claim to knowledge is, strictly speaking, false.) But if there is also a contextualist position about the semantics of 'know', and the issue between contextualist and invariantist is in principle indeterminate of outcome, then the absolutist theory of 'know' cannot be determinately right, and the argument to scepticism cannot be determinately successful—which I offer as a polite way of saying that it fails.

I have argued, however, that the absolutist reading of 'know' is mistaken: were it correct, I suggested, no debate about scepticism of the warmth which is actually found could exist. But my reason for rejecting the absolutist reading is for the moment immaterial. The question is rather, whether just by rejecting it I am not in conflict with Unger, who maintains (does he not?) that it cannot be definitively rejected: that would be definitively to reject the invariantist view of its semantics. Unger's relativism does in a sense involve the rejection of absolutism, but not in this way. He does not so much reject *it* as its claim to be determinately better than any of its rivals.

There is, or at any rate should be, no conflict here. Unfortunately Unger sometimes writes as if an invariantist view had to be absolutist (which, if it were so, would make the two terms co-extensive), but his reasons for saying this, if indeed he really wants to say it, are quite unclear to me. The invariantist says that there is a single, invariant, context-independent standard for knowledge. That is one thing; to say that it has to be the toughest standard that is even in principle possible seems to be quite another. Consider '*X* is a doctor'. An absolutist account of the meaning of that sentence might, I suppose, be something like this: *X* is so good at diagnosing and curing illness that nobody could, even in principle, be any better at it. I imagine that most of us would want to reject this account as simply wrong, or at the very least as totally arbitrary and unmotivated by anything in our thought or linguistic practice. But surely that does not bar us from thinking that 'doctor' needs an invariantist definition, for instance: a doctor is someone who has passed certain exams and so acquired certain qualifications. If you have got them you are a doctor, if you haven't you aren't; context means nothing, however grateful you might under certain circumstances be for the attentions of some medically very knowledgeable person who wasn't, however, a doctor. Invariantism without absolutism certainly seems to be an option.

Once we realise this we see that the distinction between Invariantism and Contextualism does not bear directly on the truth or falsity of scepticism. An invariantist doctrine of the semantics of 'know' might be one which set the invariant standard at some level which we all reach frequently, so that a high percentage of everyday ascriptions of knowledge turn out to be true and the claims of scepticism to be based on mere misapprehension. A contextualist, on the other hand, might be able to argue that certain features of the contexts of most of our utterances about knowledge set the (variable) standards at a higher level than we realise, with the result that very many of these utterances, maybe even whole classes of them, were actually false; he would award the sceptic a significant victory. Just how plausible he could make this line appear remains to be seen, but pending developments it has to be ranked amongst the prima facie possibilities.

On the second of these points, including the difficulties which the combined contextualist-sceptic will face, Unger is quite clear.[2] But the first he appears to have missed, for immediately before these remarks about contextualism he says that 'An invariantist account of 'know' will *directly* give the day to scepticism about knowledge, at least to a fairly extreme form of that view' (original italics). This

[2] Ibid., p. 51 l.11 ff.

implies the equation of an invariantist with an absolutist account, something which is also implied earlier.[3] Now some will read this earlier passage as more than an implication. This (they will rightly say) is where Unger introduces the term 'invariantism', so we have not an implication but a definition: Unger means invariantism to be the same doctrine as what he in his earlier work called absolutism.

That may be so, though I doubt it. But if it is, I would observe that there is room for a doctrine which is neither contextualism, nor that proposed by Dretske which Unger also discusses,[4] nor invariantism as Unger seems to introduce the word, that is, as synonymous with absolutism. This doctrine is what I have up to now been calling 'invariantism', which seems a good word for it in view of its content: an invariantist with respect to a certain expression gives its semantics in terms of a single, context-invariant, standard. Absolutism is one type of invariantism, but only one type, and we might therefore declare an absolutist account of some expression simply false without implying that any invariantist account of it would be simply false and some contextualist account of it true. Unger's Semantic Relativism, the idea that for many expressions there are plausible semantics of both invariantist and contextualist stamp such that no matter of fact could decide the issue between them, can still be accepted.

But isn't there still some kind of clash between my procedure and Semantic Relativism? I have spoken (in Section XI and elsewhere) as if the semantics of 'know' were invariant, and the questions to be answered were simply: what is the invariant standard which captures them, and why is that the standard we arrive at? Much use was made, it is true, of the notion of contextually determined standards, but that was because we started our thought-experiment from the subjective standpoint of the individual with his own particular interests and situation in order to see how the process of 'objectivisation' leads to a concept whose conditions of application are intersubjective and far more narrowly circumscribed. Am I not then found to be maintaining something which can be true—meaning determinately true—only if Unger's Semantic Relativism is false?

Again, I think not; the impression of disagreement is superficial. Readers of Unger's *Philosophical Relativity* will recall that in the

---

[3] Ibid., p. 9 l.10–12.   [4] Ibid., pp. 30–3.

case of any particular utterance there are various things which are agreed between invariantist and contextualist. They are agreed that there is a certain thought on which the speaker brings the hearers to focus; what they disagree on are the roles played, in the process by which he does this, by the semantics of his words on the one hand and the pragmatics of the situation on the other. But if they are agreed on that, there can hardly be any difficulty of principle for them in agreeing that there may be some expressions which are characteristically used to fix attention on pretty much the same thought (here in the sense: the same stringency of standard) in all contexts of utterance. Whether a particular expression is like this or not may be contentious; whether 'know' behaves in this way may be a point of disagreement between myself and Unger—though more of that in a moment. But contextualist and invariantist as such are not committed either to the view that there are, or that there are not, such expressions.

What can be said is that if some particular expression is agreed to be of this type, a contextualist account of it will look a somewhat round about way of reaching the place which an invariantist reaches in one step. But even if there were simply no hope for the contextualist view in such a case there would be no conflict with Semantic Relativism. For that doctrine, if I understand it correctly, tells us that where a range of standards is in use the phenomena can be equally well explained on invariantist and contextualist models. Of expressions which are not associated with a range but with only with one, invariant standard, it tells us nothing, leaving us free to conclude that there the balance tips towards invariantism. But in any case it is not true that my account of 'know' leaves nothing that contextualism can usefully do, and that for two reasons.

The first involves an indirect use of the basic contextualist idea. It is exactly the use that I have already made of it, though not under that name. What we were considering in Section X (on 'Objectivisation') was the way in which contexts, constituted by varieties of need, prospective outcomes, recognitional capacities, levels of ignorance of prevailing conditions, and so on, guide our assessment of sources of information. And it was a feature of these contexts—principally, the fact that one often does not know what the information is needed for, or will later be used for, or what will turn on its use—that created an obvious role for a concept tied to some high standard of reliability. So the contextualist has certainly had his share of the action, even if that action results in a situation for which, some might think, only the invariantist need apply.

The second point is more straightforward. To say that knowledge always implies a very high level of reliability is not to say that the level is always the same. Many everyday claims to knowledge are allowed to get by although made with thinner support than many others, which, occurring in different circumstances, are questioned and even rejected. Looking at the cases in which we are apparently laxer, the invariantist can say that these knowledge-claims are false but that we judge according to context what degree of departure from strict truth is appropriate and acceptable; the contextualist can say that they may well be true, since context affects the details of their semantics. On the question which position, if either, is right, I am happy to follow Unger's powerfully argued recommendation. My 'practical explication' or 'state of nature' method leads to an account of the linguistic practice surrounding the word 'know' and its near relatives; it does not determine how we are to apportion the underlying mechanics of the practice between invariant semantics and contextually motivated pragmatics.

REFERENCES

Armstrong, D. M., *Belief, Truth and Knowledge* (Cambridge University Press, 1973).

Austin, J. L., 'Other Minds', in *Philosophical Papers*, ed. Urmson and Warnock (Oxford, Clarendon Press, 1961).

Blackburn, S. W., 'Knowledge, Truth and Reliability', in *Proceedings of the British Academy*, lxx (1984), 167–87.

Craig, E. J. (1) 'The Practical Explication of Knowledge', in *Proceedings of the Aristotelian Society*, (1986–7), 211–26.

—— (2) *The Mind of God and the Works of Man* (Oxford, Clarendon Press, 1987).

—— (3) 'Nozick and the Sceptic: the Thumbnail Version', in *Analysis*, vol. 49 (1989), 161–2.

Descartes, R., *Meditations on First Philosophy*, in *The Philosophical Writings of Descartes* Vol. II trans. Cottingham, Stoothoff and Murdoch (Cambridge University Press, 1984), 3–62.

Dretske, F., 'Conclusive Reasons', in *Australasian Journal of Philosophy* xlix (1971), 1–22.

Edwards, P., 'Bertrand Russell's Doubts about Induction', in *Logic and Language* (First Series), ed. Flew (Oxford, Basil Blackwell, 1960).

Forbes, G., 'Nozick and the Sceptic', in *Philosophical Quarterly*, xxxiv (1984), 43–52.

Gettier, E., 'Is Justified True Belief Knowledge?' in *Analysis*, xxiii (1963), 121–3.

Goldman, A. (1) 'A Causal Theory of Knowing', in *Journal of Philosophy*, lxiv (1967), 357–72.

—— (2) 'Discrimination and Perceptual Knowledge', in ibid., lxxiii (1976), 771–91.

Grice, H. P. 'Logic and Conversation', appended to *Understanding Arguments* by R. J. Fogelin (Harcourt Brace Jovanovich, 1978), 329–42.

Harman, G., *Thought* (Princeton University Press, 1973).

Hintikka, J., *Knowledge and Belief* (Cornell University Press, 1962).

Hume, D., *An Enquiry Concerning Human Understanding*, 3rd edn., ed. Selby-Bigge, rev. Nidditch (Oxford, Clarendon Press, 1975).

Lehrer, K., 'Knowledge, Truth and Evidence', in *Analysis*, xxv (1964–5), 168–75.

Lewis, D. K., *Counterfactuals* (Oxford, Basil Blackwell, 1973).

McGinn, C., 'The Concept of Knowledge', in *Midwest Studies in Philosophy*, ix (1984), 529–54.

Moore, G. E. 'A Defence of Common Sense', in *Philosophical Papers* (London, George Allen and Unwin, 1959), 32–59.

Nozick, R. (1) *Anarchy, State and Utopia* (Oxford, Basil Blackwell, 1974).

—— (2) *Philosophical Explanations* (Oxford, Clarendon Press, 1981).

Pascal, B., *Pensées*, trans. Krailsheimer (Penguin, 1966).

Pears, D. F., *What is Knowledge?* (London, George Allen and Unwin, 1972).

Plato, *Meno*, trans. Guthrie (Penguin, 1956).

Radford, C., 'Knowledge—by examples', in *Analysis*, xxvii (1966–7), 1–11.

Ramsey, F. P., 'Knowledge', in *Foundations: Essays in Philosophy, Logic, Mathematics and Economics*, ed. Mellor (London, Routledge and Kegan Paul, 1978), 126–7.

Ross, A., 'Why do we believe what we are told?' in *Ratio*, xxviii (1986), 69–88.

Ryle, G., *The Concept of Mind* (Hutchinson, 1949).

Schopenhauer, A., *On the Fourfold Root of the Principle of Sufficient Reason*.

Unger, P. (1) 'An Analysis of Factual Knowledge', in *Journal of Philosophy*, (1968), 157–70.

—— (2) 'A Defence of Skepticism', in *Philosophical Review*, (1971), 198–219.

—— (3) *Ignorance—a Case for Scepticism* (Oxford, Clarendon Press, 1975).

—— (4) *Philosophical Relativity* (Oxford, Basil Blackwell, 1984).

Welbourne, M., *The Community of Knowledge* (Aberdeen University Press, 1986).

Williams, B. A. O. (1) 'Knowledge and Reasons', in *Problems in the Theory of Knowledge*, ed. von Wright (The Hague, Martinus Nijhoff, 1972), 1–11.

—— (2) *Descartes: the Project of Pure Enquiry* (Penguin, 1978).

INDEX OF NAMES